REVISED AND EXPANDED EDITION

FINGERPICKING
BEATLES

P9-DME-244

Cover photo provided by London Features International

ISBN 0-7935-7051-4

HAL•LEONARD®
CORPORATION

7777 W. BLUEMOUND RD. P.O. BOX 13819 MILWAUKEE, WI 53213

Visit Hal Leonard Online at
www.halleonard.com

INTRODUCTION TO FINGERSTYLE GUITAR

Fingerstyle (a.k.a. fingerpicking) is a guitar technique that means you literally pick the strings with your right-hand fingers and thumb. This contrasts with the conventional technique of strumming and playing single notes with a pick (a.k.a. flatpicking). For fingerpicking, you can use any type of guitar: acoustic steel-string, nylon-string classical, or electric.

THE RIGHT HAND

The most common right-hand position is shown below:

Use a high wrist; arch your palm as if you were holding a ping-pong ball. Keep the thumb outside and away from the fingers, and let the fingers do the work rather than lifting your whole hand.

The thumb generally plucks the bottom strings with downstrokes on the left side of the thumb and thumbnail. The other fingers pluck the higher strings using upstokes with the fleshy tip of the fingers and fingernails. The thumb and fingers should pluck one string per stroke and not brush over several strings.

Another picking option you may choose to use is called **hybrid picking** (a.k.a. plectrum-style fingerpicking). Here, the pick is usually held between the thumb and first finger, and the three remaining fingers are assigned to pluck the higher strings.

THE LEFT HAND

The left-hand fingers are numbered 1 though 4:

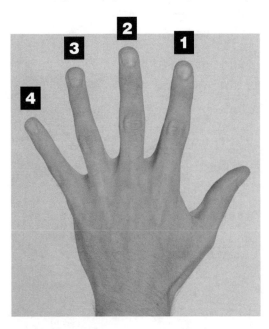

Be sure to keep your fingers arched, with each joint bent; if they flatten out across the strings, they will deaden the sound when you fingerpick. As a general rule, let the strings ring as long as possible when playing fingerstyle.

Across the Universe

Words and Music by John Lennon and Paul McCartney

Drop D tuning:
(low to high) D-A-D-G-B-E

Intro
Slowly

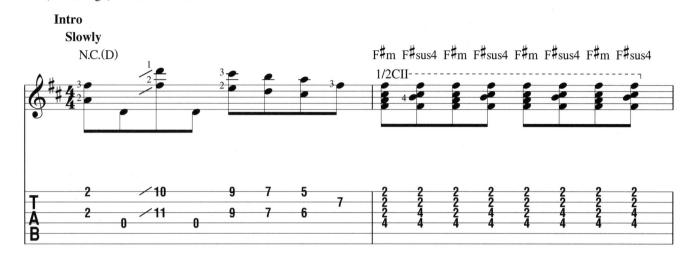

Verse

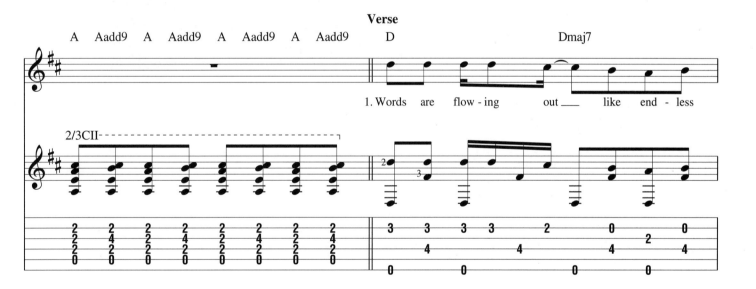

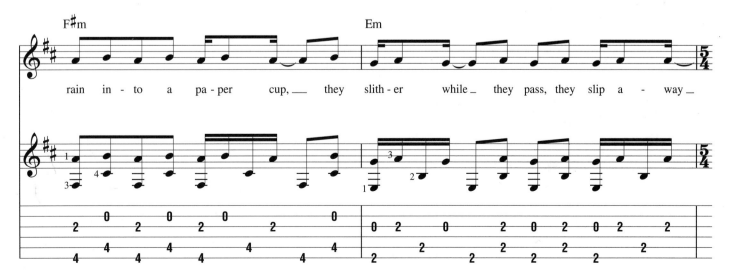

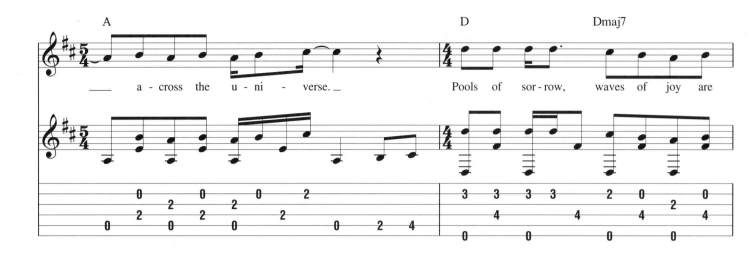

across the u-ni-verse. Pools of sor-row, waves of joy are

drift-ing through my o-pen mind, _ pos-sess-ing and ca-ress-ing me. _

𝄋 Chorus

Jai_ Gu-ru_____ De - va. _ Om.

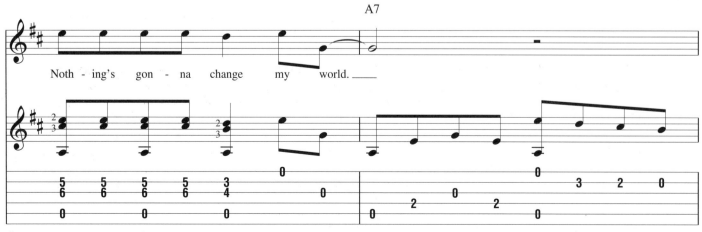

Noth-ing's gon-na change my world. ___

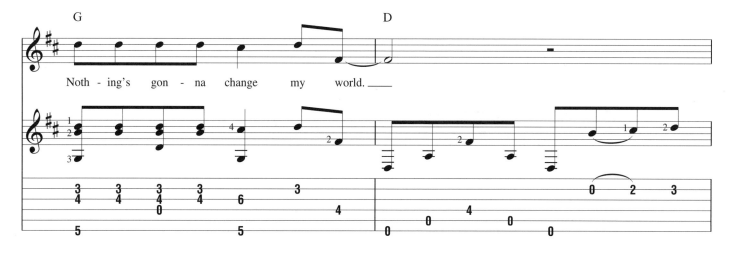

Noth - ing's gon - na change my world. ____

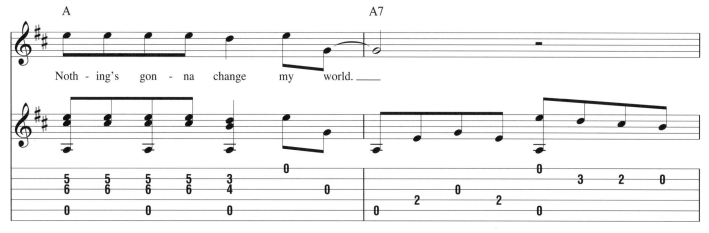

Noth - ing's gon - na change my world. ____

To Coda 1

To Coda 2

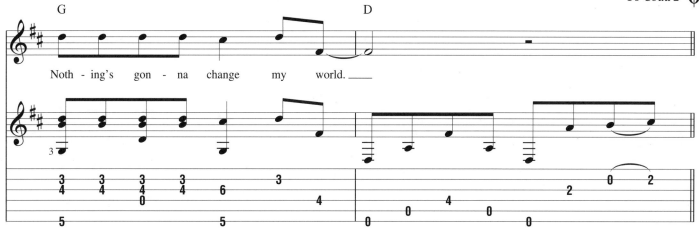

Noth - ing's gon - na change my world. ____

Verse

2. Im - ag - es ____ of bro - ken light which dance be - fore ____ me like a mil - ion eyes, __

5

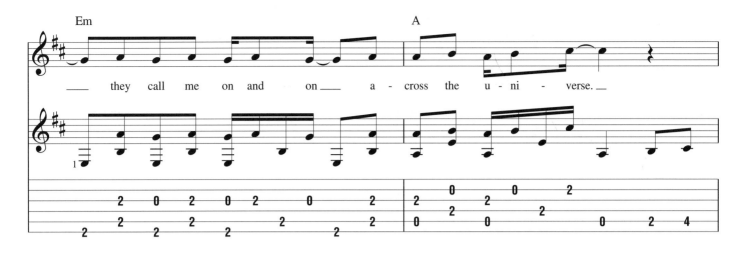

_____ they call me on and on _____ a - cross the u - ni - verse. _____

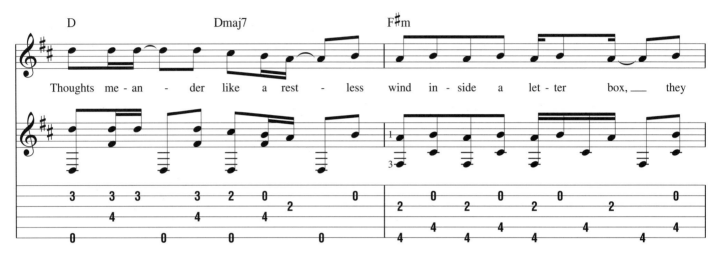

Thoughts me - an - der like a rest - less wind in - side a let - ter box, _____ they

D.S. al Coda 1

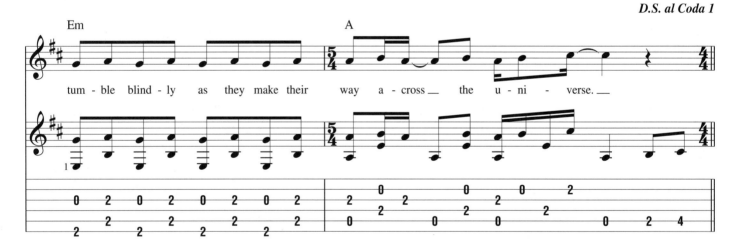

tum - ble blind - ly as they make their way a - cross _____ the u - ni - verse. _____

Coda 1
Verse

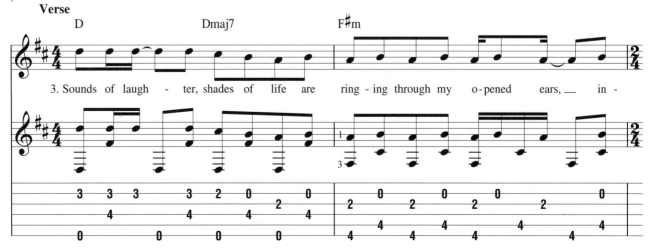

3. Sounds of laugh - ter, shades of life are ring - ing through my o - pened ears, _____ in -

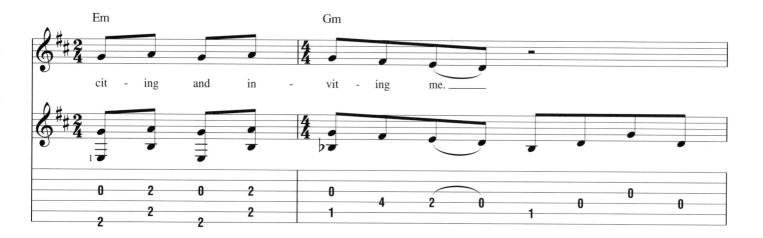

cit - ing and in - vit - ing me. ____

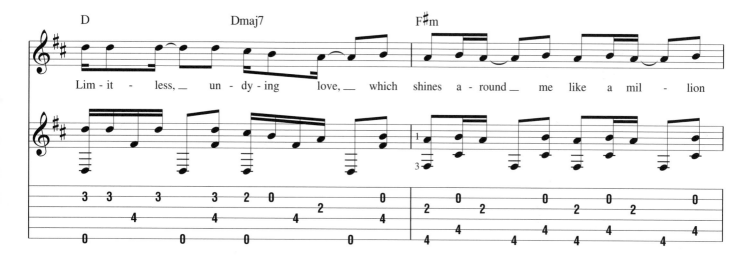

Lim - it - less, __ un - dy - ing love, __ which shines a - round __ me like a mil - lion

D.S. al Coda 2

suns, and calls me on and on ___ a - cross the u - ni - verse. __

Coda 2
Outro

Jai ___ Gu - ru ____ De - va. __

7

All You Need Is Love

Words and Music by John Lennon and Paul McCartney

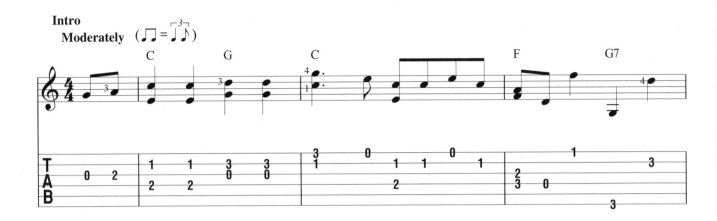

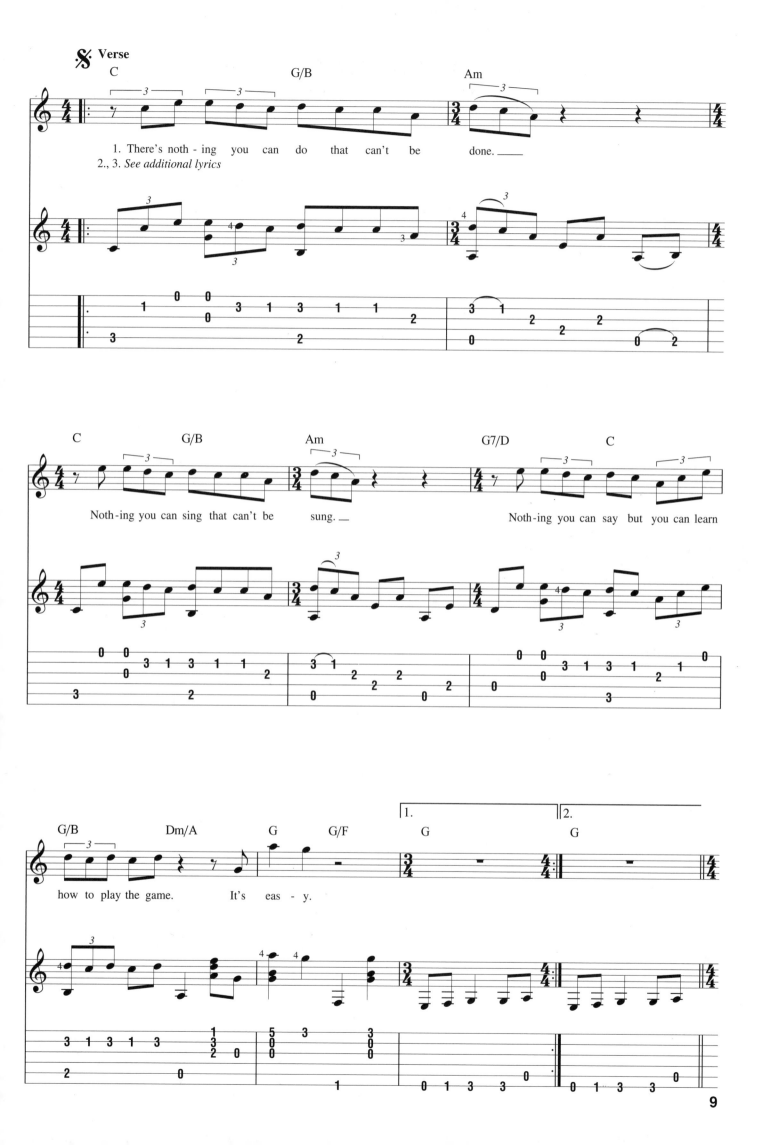

Verse

1. There's noth-ing you can do that can't be done. ___

2., 3. *See additional lyrics*

Noth-ing you can sing that can't be sung. ___ Noth-ing you can say but you can learn

how to play the game. It's eas-y.

9

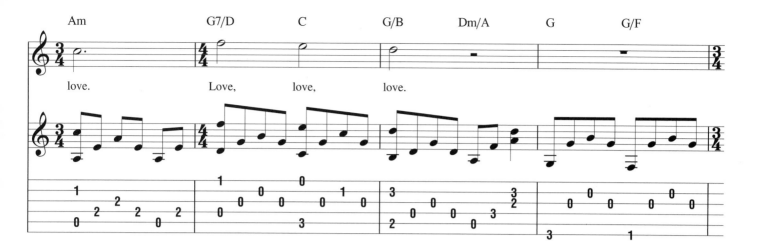

love.   Love,   love,   love.

Chorus

All   you   need   is   love. ____

All   you   need   is   love. ____   All   you   need   is   love, __

D.S. al Coda
(take 2nd ending)

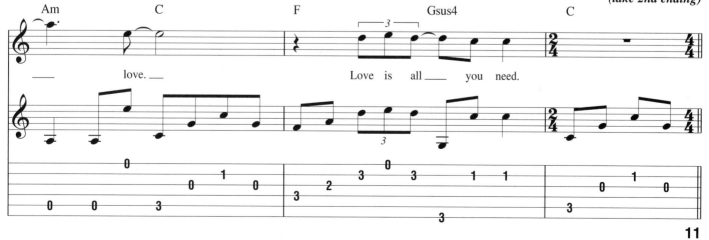

____   love. __   Love   is   all ____   you   need.

Coda

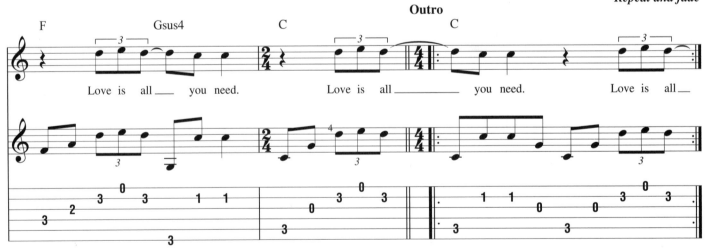

Additional Lyrics

2. Nothing you can make that can't be made.
   No one you can save that can't be saved.
   Nothing you can do, but you can learn how to be you in time.
   It's easy.

3. There's nothing you can know that isn't known.
   Nothing you can see that isn't shown.
   Nowhere you can be that isn't where you're meant to be.
   It's easy.

And I Love Her

Words and Music by John Lennon and Paul McCartney

Intro
Moderately

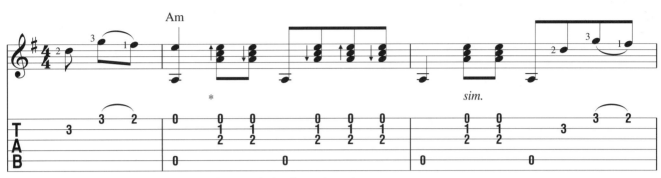

*Strum w/ index finger throughout

1. I give her all my love, __
2., 3. *See additional lyrics*

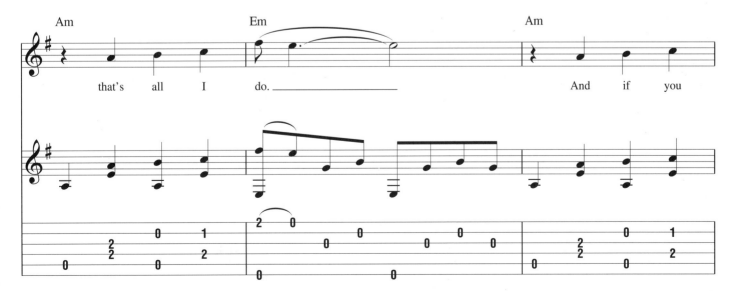

that's all I do. _____ And if you

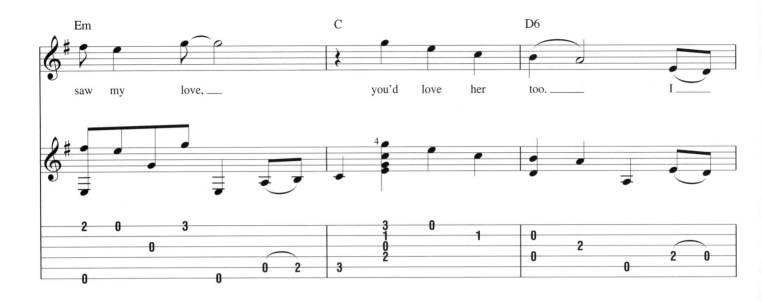

saw my love, ___ you'd love her too. ___ I ___

1.

2.

To Coda ⊕

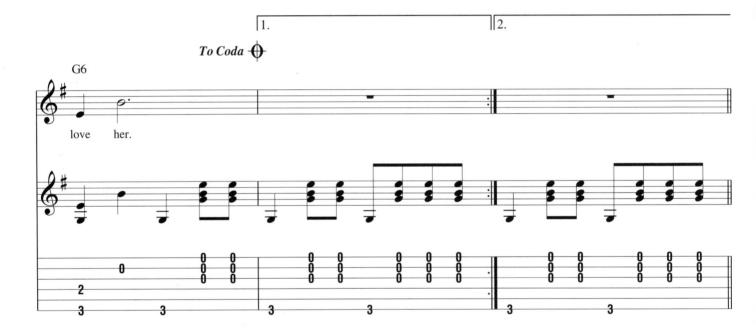

love her.

Bridge

A love like ours ___ could nev-er die, ___

14

as long as I _____ have you near me. _____

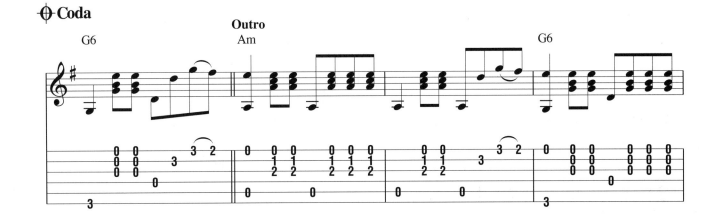

⊕ Coda

Outro

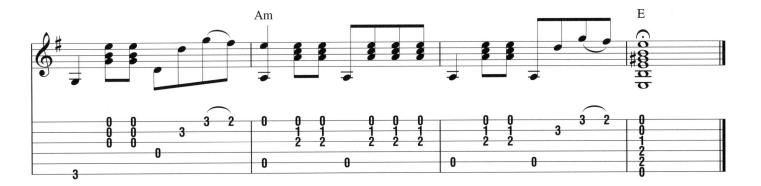

Additional Lyrics

2. She gives me ev'rything,
   And tenderly.
   The kiss my lover brings,
   She brings to me,
   And I love her.

3. Bright are the stars that shine,
   Dark is the sky,
   I know this love of mine
   Will never die,
   And I love her.

Blackbird

Words and Music by John Lennon and Paul McCartney

*Guitar part is an arrangement of recorded version and does not contain melody notes.

1., 3. Black - bird sing - ing in the dead of night,
2. Black - bird sing - ing in the dead of night,

take these bro - ken wings ___ and learn to fly. ___
take these sunk - en eyes ___ and learn to see. ___

All your ___ life, ___
All your ___ life, ___

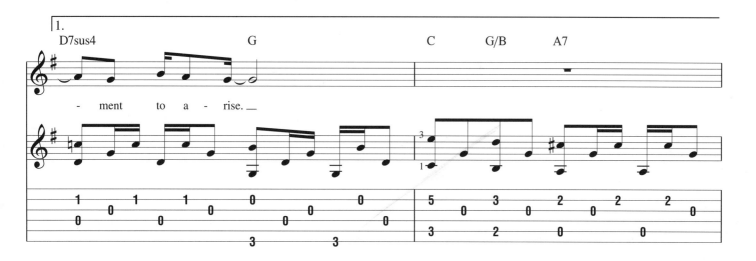

you were on - ly wait - ing for this mo -
you were on - ly wait - ing for this mo -

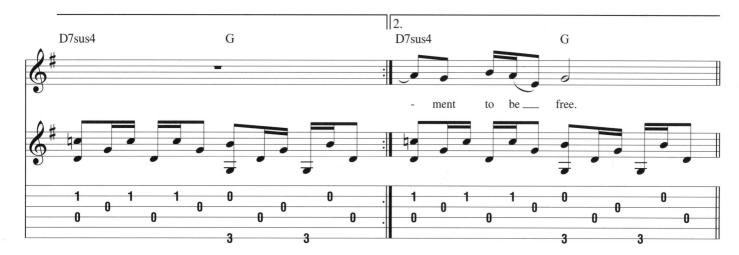

1.

- ment to a - rise. ___

2.

- ment to be ___ free.

𝄋 Bridge

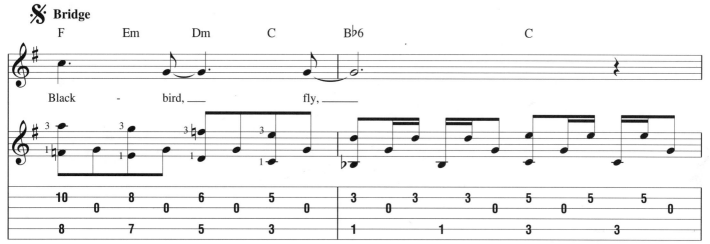

Black - bird, ___ fly, ___

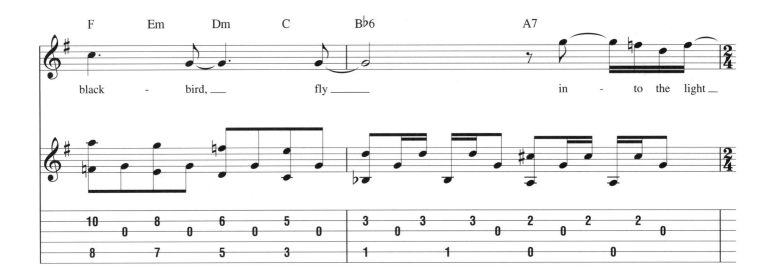

black - bird, ___ fly _____ in - to the light ___

To Coda 1 ⊕

Interlude

___ of the dark black _____ night. __

D.S. al Coda 1

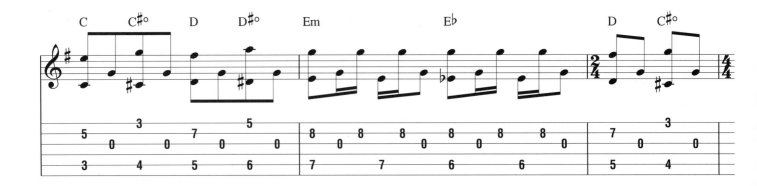

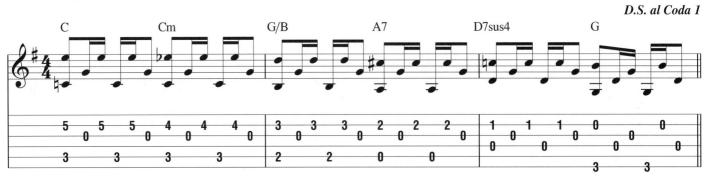

Coda 1

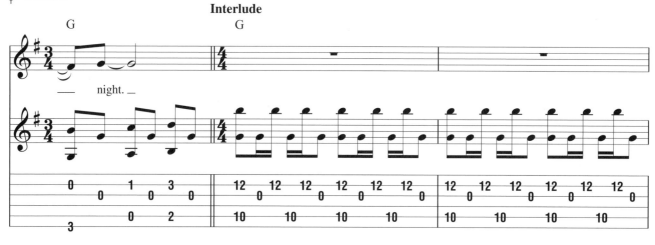

Interlude

night.

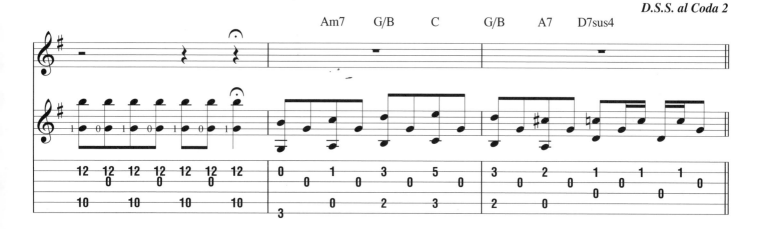

D.S.S. al Coda 2

 Coda 2

Outro

- ment to a - rise. You were on - ly __ wait-ing for this mo -

- ment to a - rise. You were on - ly __ wait-ing for this mo - ment to a - rise.

Can't Buy Me Love

Words and Music by John Lennon and Paul McCartney

get you an-y - thing, ___ my friend, if it makes you feel al - right. ___

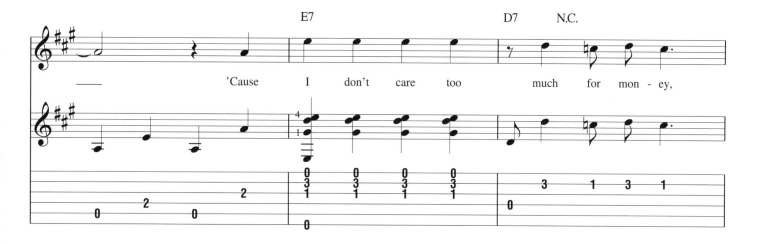

___ 'Cause I don't care too much for mon - ey,

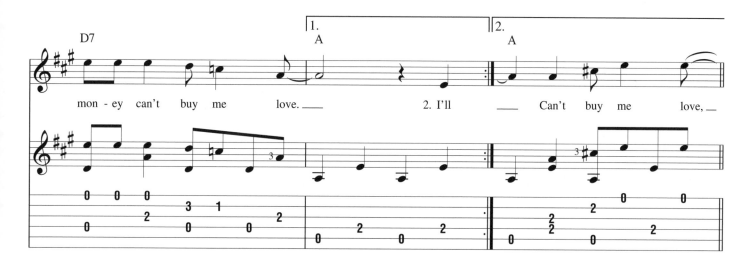

mon - ey can't buy me love. ___   2. I'll   ___   Can't buy me love, ___

𝄋 **Chorus**

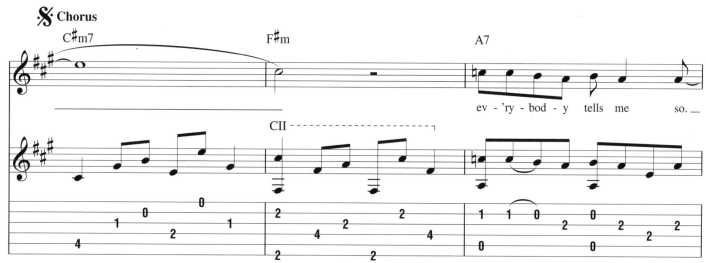

ev - 'ry - bod - y tells me   so. ___

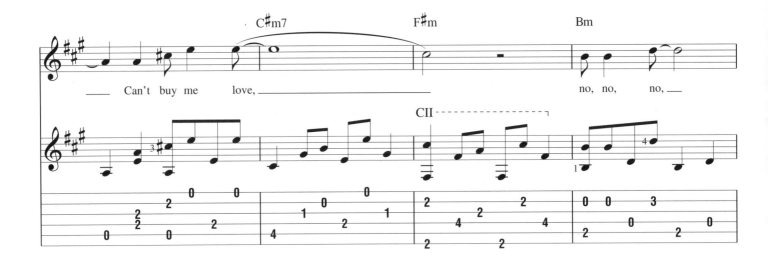

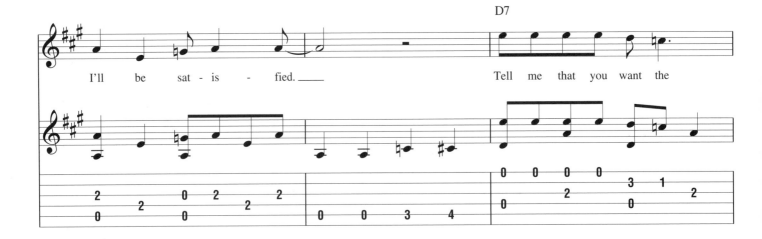

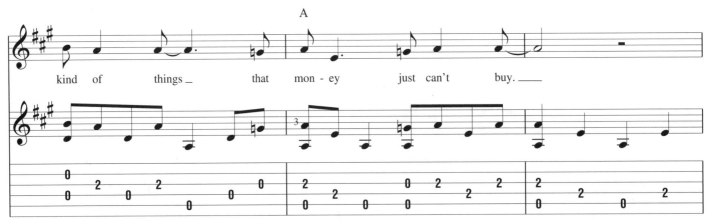

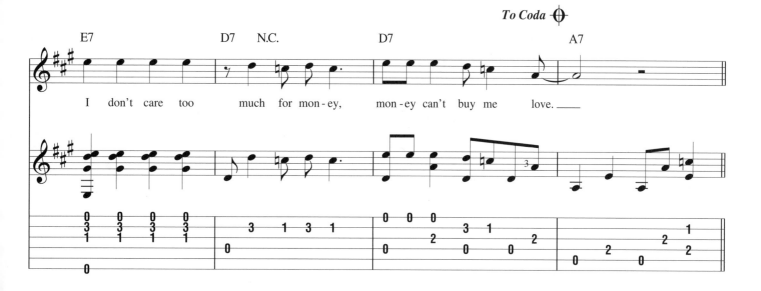

I don't care too much for mon-ey, mon-ey can't buy me love. ____

Guitar Solo

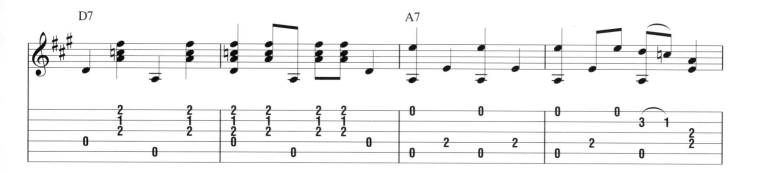

Can't buy me love____

Coda

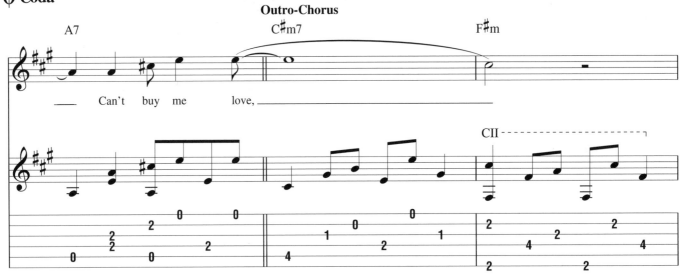

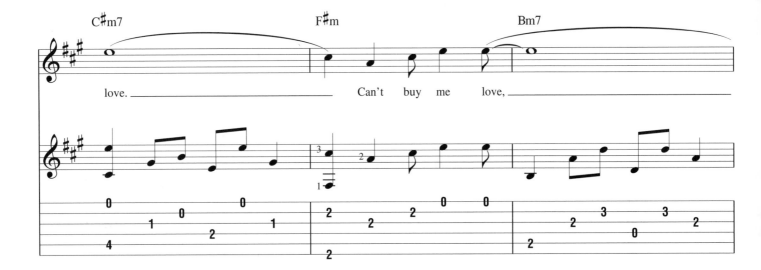

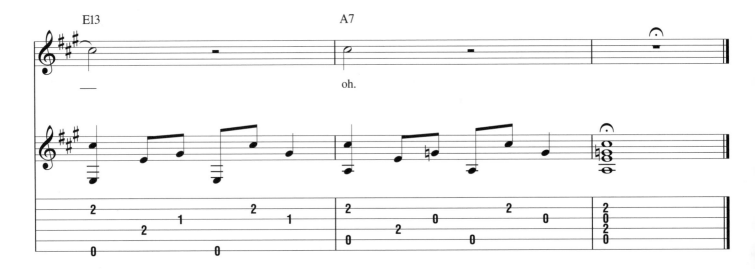

Additional Lyrics

2. I'll give you all I got to give
If you say you love me too.
I may not have a lot to give
But what I got I'll give to you.
I don't care too much for money,
Money can't buy me love.

Dear Prudence

Words and Music by John Lennon and Paul McCartney

Drop D tuning:
(low to high) D-A-D-G-B-E

Intro

Moderately slow

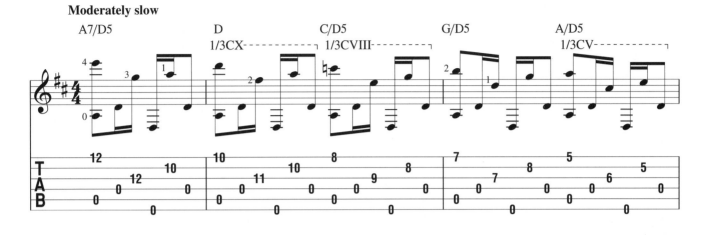

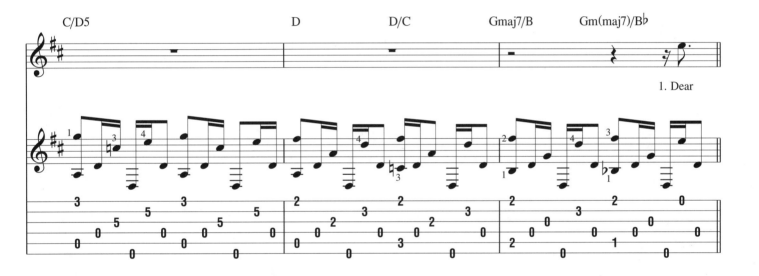

1. Dear

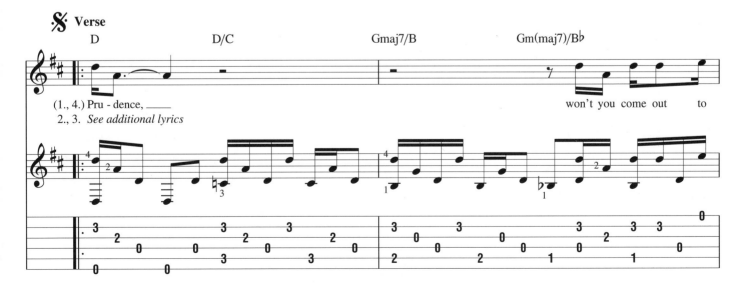

(1., 4.) Pru - dence, ___

2., 3. *See additional lyrics*

won't you come out to

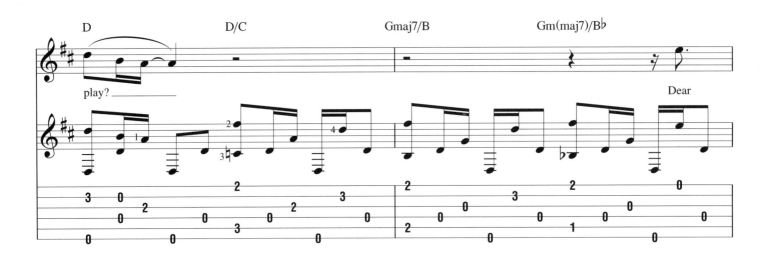

play? _____   Dear

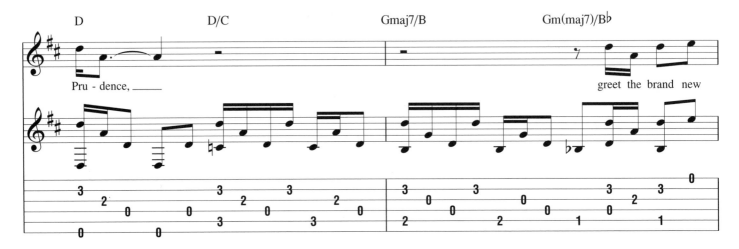

Pru - dence, _____   greet the brand new

4th time, To Coda ⊕

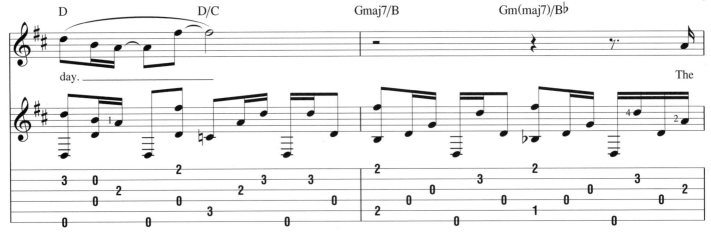

day. _____   The

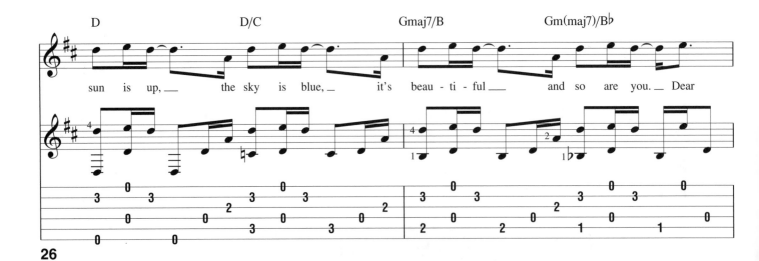

sun is up, ___ the sky is blue, ___ it's beau - ti - ful ___ and so are you. ___ Dear

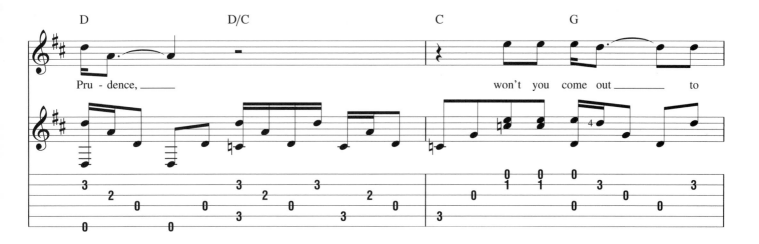

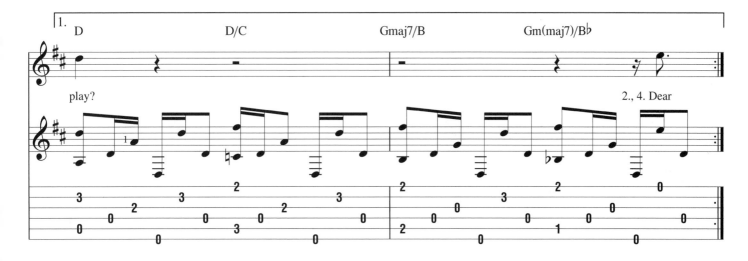

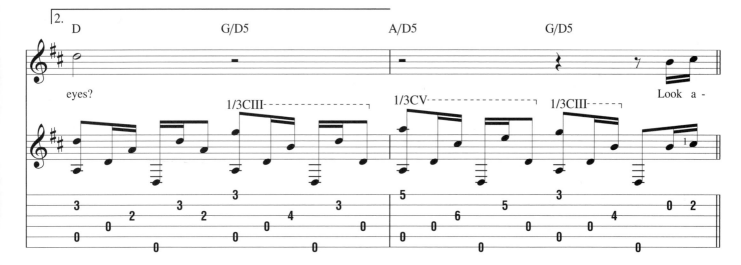

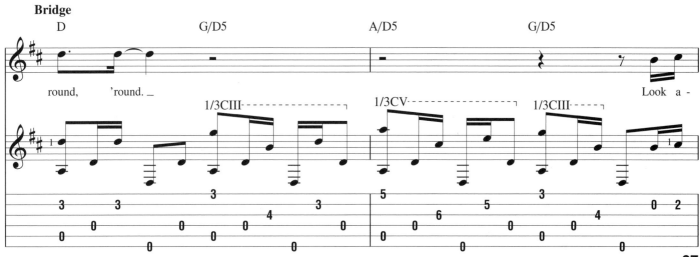

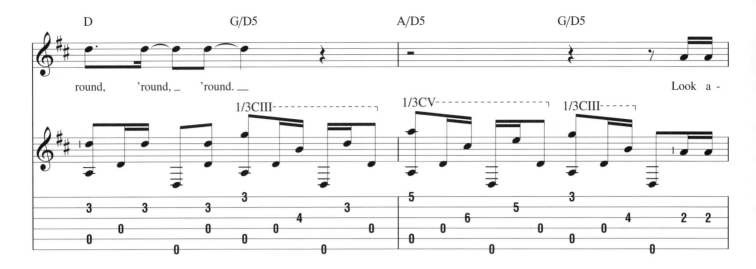

round,   'round, _   'round. _   Look a-

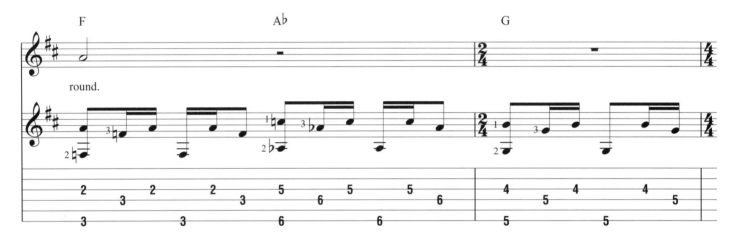

round.

D.S. al Coda
(take repeat)

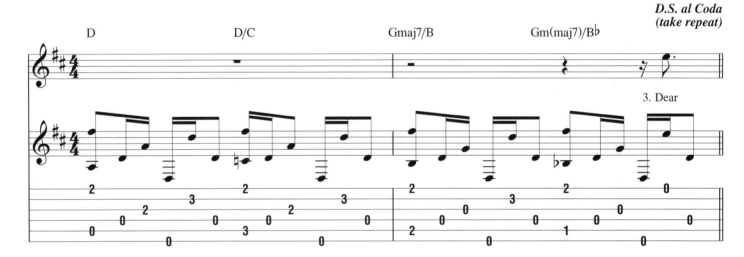

3. Dear

⊕ Coda

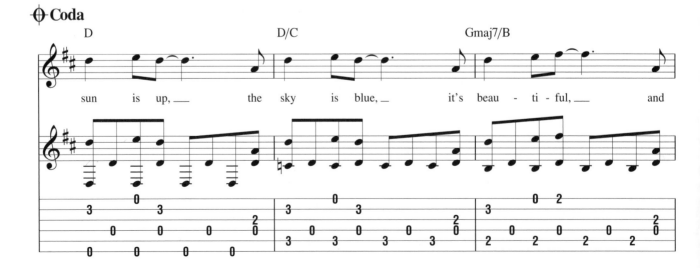

sun is up, ___   the sky is blue, ___   it's beau - ti - ful, ___   and

so are you. __ Dear Pru - dence, won't you come out __ to

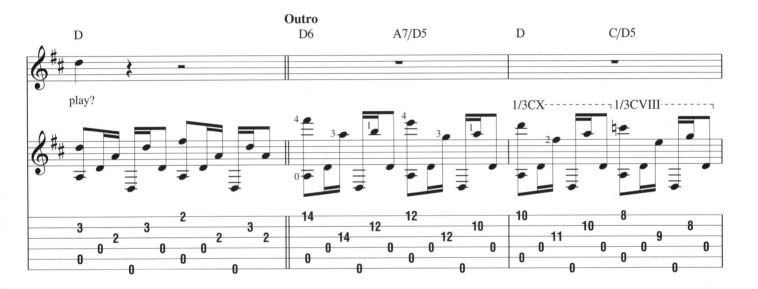

Outro

play?

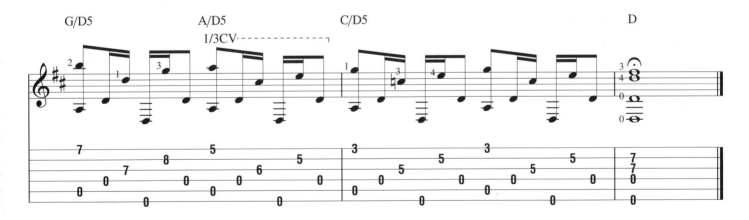

Additional Lyrics

2. Dear Prudence, open up your eyes.
   Dear Prudence, see the sunny skies.
   The wind is low. The birds will sing
   That you are part of everything.
   Dear Prudence, won't you open up your eyes?

3. Dear Prudence, let me see you smile.
   Dear Prudence, like a little child.
   The clouds will be a daisy chain,
   So let me see you smile again.
   Dear Prudence, won't you let me see you smile?

A Day in the Life

Words and Music by John Lennon and Paul McCartney

2. He blew his mind ___ out in a car.
3., 4. *See additional lyrics*

He did - n't no - tice that the lights had changed. ___

A crowd of peo - ple stood and stared.

They'd seen his face be - fore. ___ No - bod - y was real - ly sure if he was from the House of

31

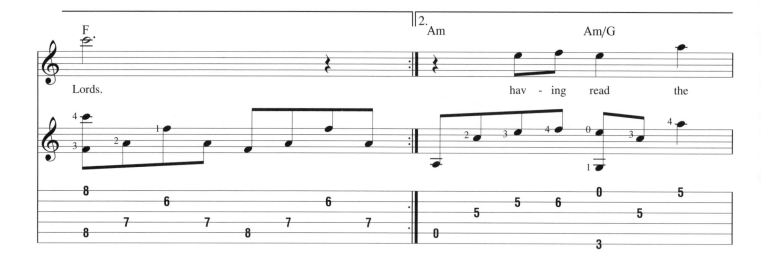

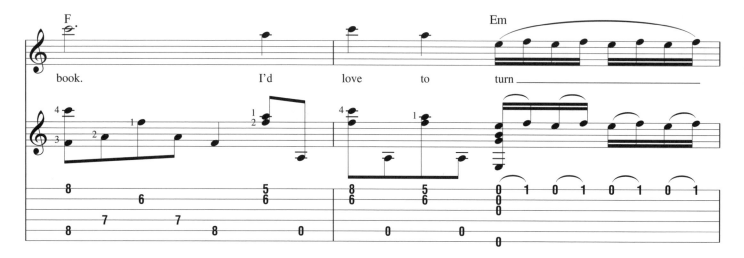

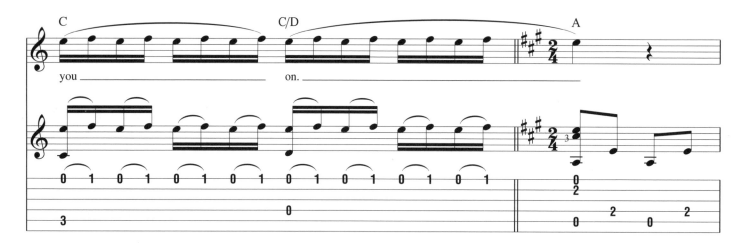

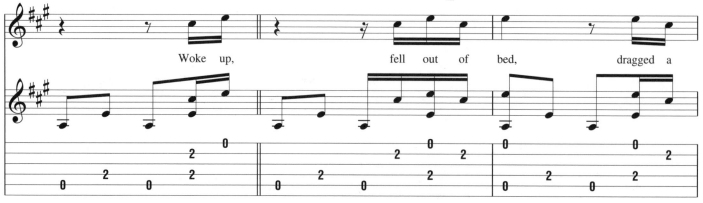

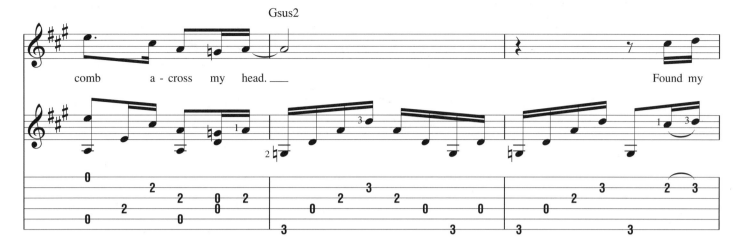

comb a - cross my head. ___ Found my

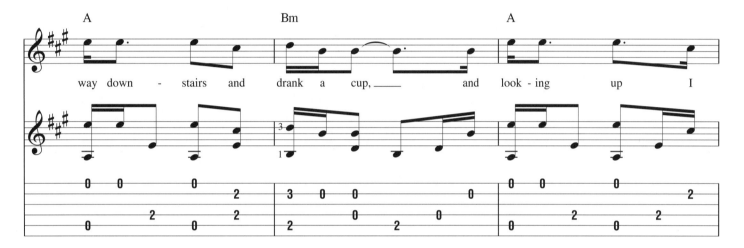

way down - stairs and drank a cup, ___ and look - ing up I

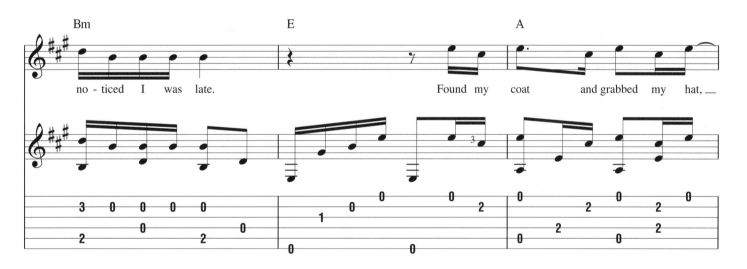

no - ticed I was late. Found my coat and grabbed my hat, ___

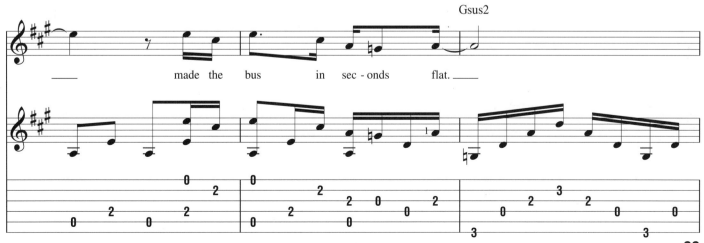

___ made the bus in sec - onds flat. ___

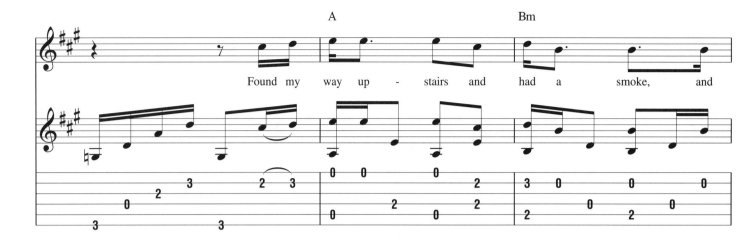

Found my way up - stairs and had a smoke, and

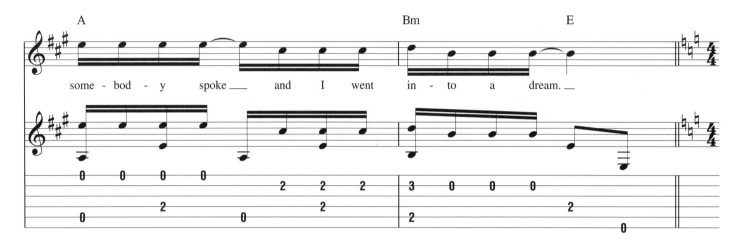

some - bod - y spoke ____ and I went in - to a dream. ____

Interlude

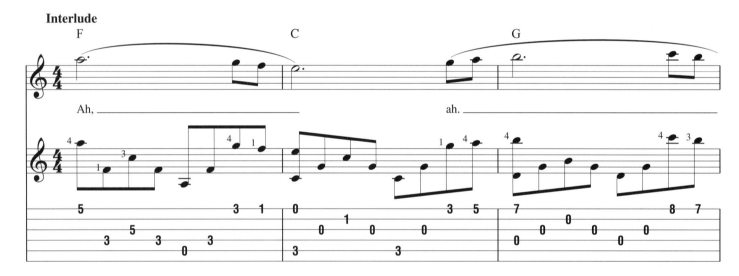

Ah, _____ ah. ____

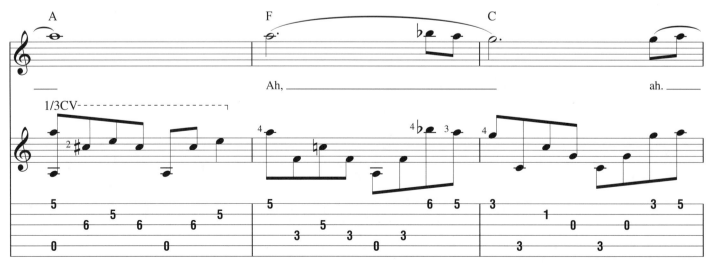

____ Ah, _____ ah. ____

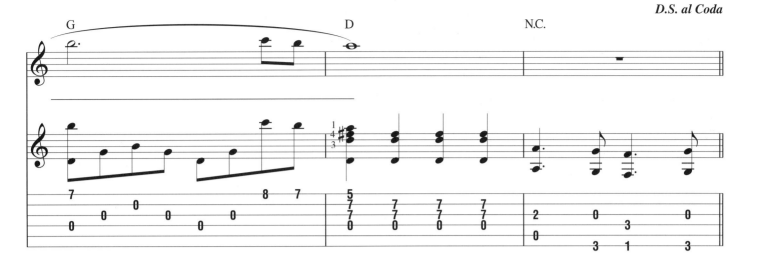

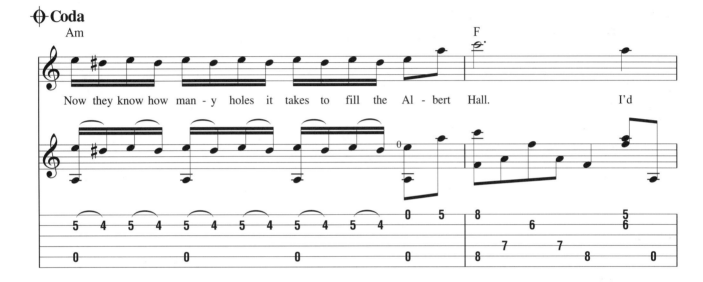

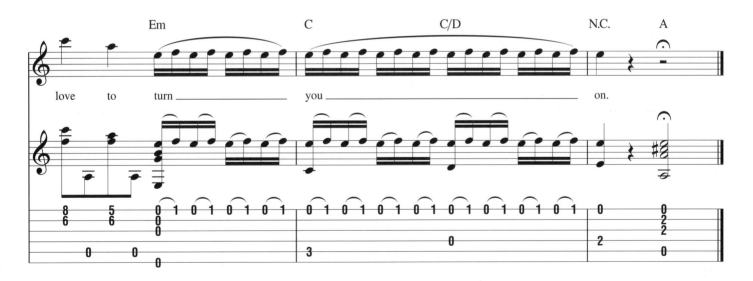

Additional Lyrics

3. I saw a film today, oh boy.
   The English army had just won the war.
   A crowd of people turned away.
   But, I just had a look,
   Having read the book.
   I'd love to turn you on.

4. I read the news today, oh boy.
   Four thousand holes in Blackburn, Lancashire.
   And though the holes were rather small,
   They had to count them all.
   Now they know how many holes it takes to fill the Albert Hall.
   I'd love to turn you on.

Eleanor Rigby

Words and Music by John Lennon and Paul McCartney

Drop D tuning:
(low to high) D-A-D-G-B-E

Intro-Chorus

Moderately

Ah, _____ look at all _____ the lone - ly peo - ple. _____

Verse

1. El - ea - nor Rig - by picks up the rice _____ in the church _____
2., 3. *See additional Lyrics*

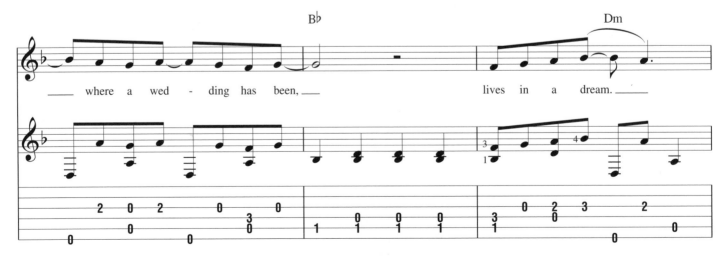

_____ where a wed - ding has been, _____ lives in a dream. _____

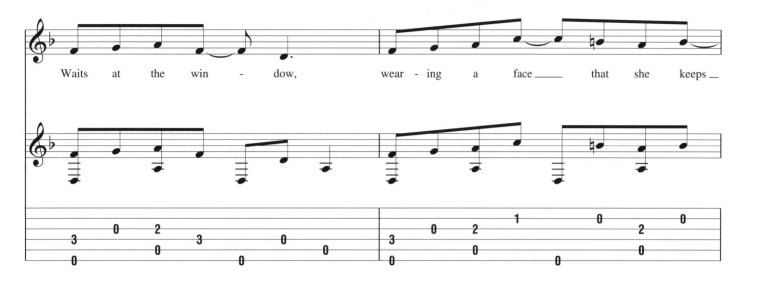

Waits at the win - dow, wear - ing a face ___ that she keeps ___

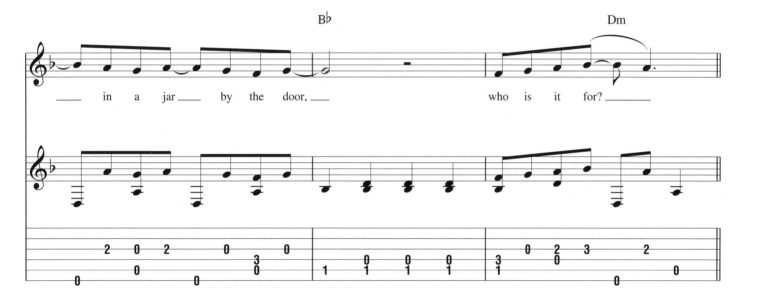

B♭   Dm

___ in a jar ___ by the door, ___   who is it for? ___

Chorus

Dm7   Dm6   B♭/D

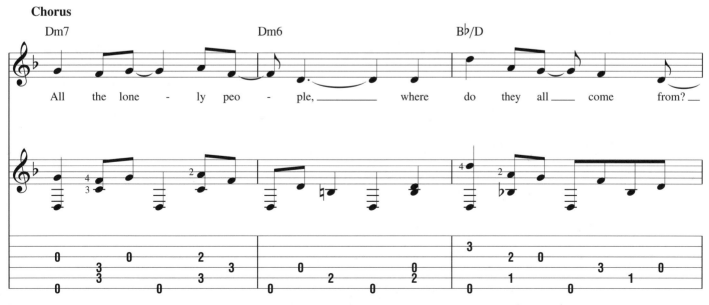

All the lone - ly peo - ple, ___ where do they all ___ come from? ___

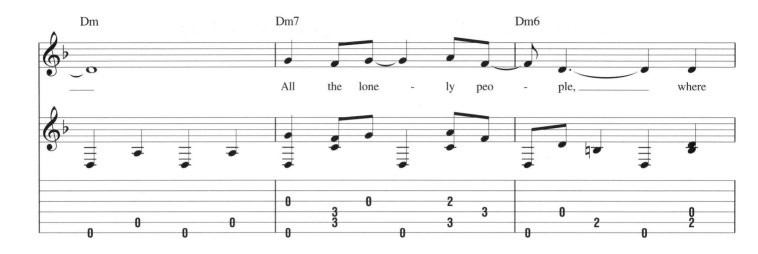

All the lone - ly peo - ple, _____ where

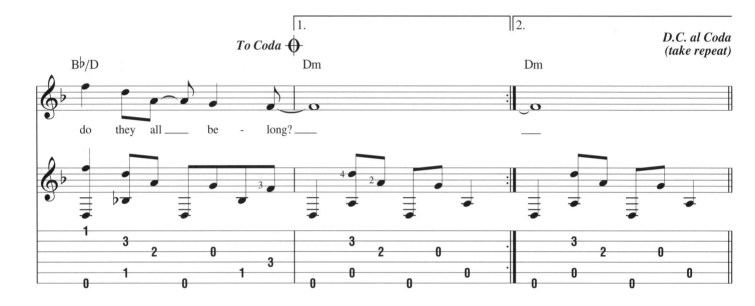

do they all ___ be - long? ___

To Coda

D.C. al Coda
(take repeat)

Coda

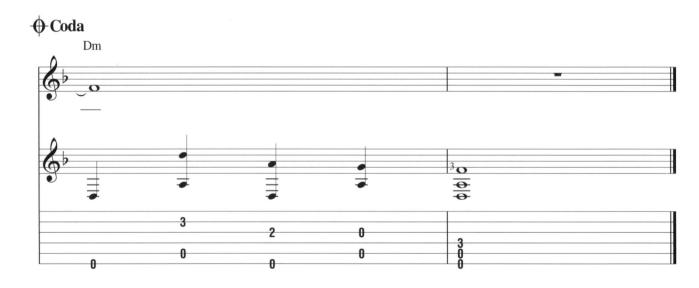

Additional Lyrics

2. Father McKenzie, writing the words of a sermon that no one will hear,
   No one comes near.
   Look at him working, darning his socks in the night when there's nobody there.
   What does he care?

3. Eleanor Rigby died in the church and was buried along with her name,
   Nobody came.
   Father McKenzie, wiping the dirt from his hands as he walks from the grave,
   No one was saved.

Here, There and Everywhere

Words and Music by John Lennon and Paul McCartney

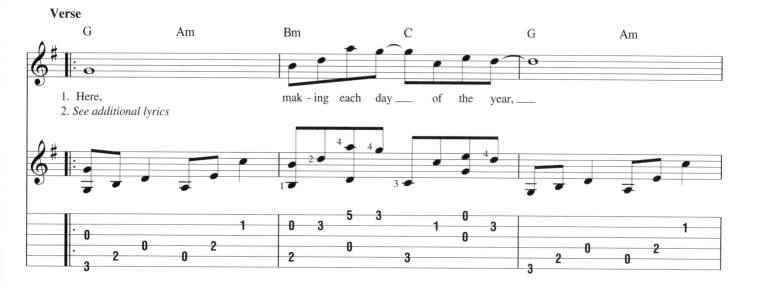

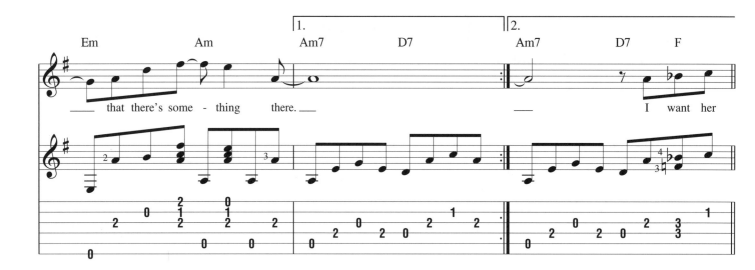

that there's some - thing there. ___

I want her

Bridge

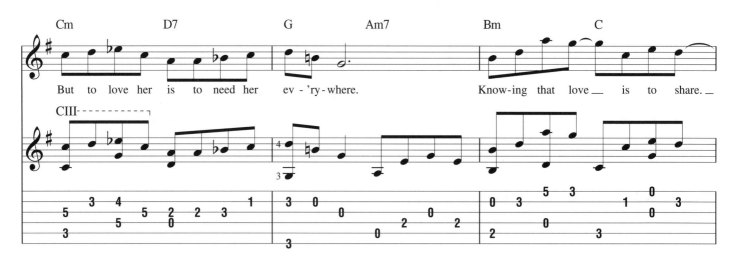

ev - 'ry - where,

and if she's be - side me I know I need nev - er care.

But to love her is to need her ev - 'ry - where.

Know-ing that love ___ is to share. ___

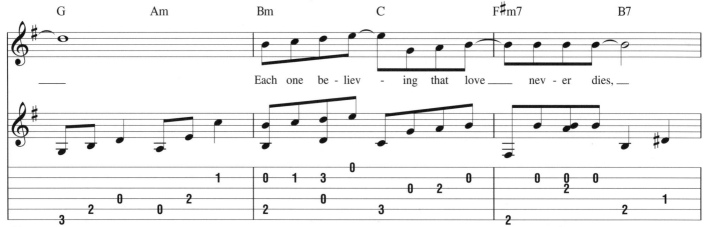

___

Each one be - liev - ing that love ___ nev - er dies, ___

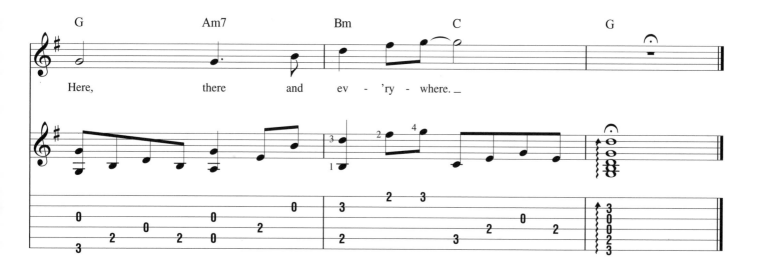

Additional Lyrics

2. There, running my hands through her hair,
Both of thinking how good it can be.
Someone is speaking,
But she doesn't know he's there.

Free As a Bird

Words and Music by John Lennon, Paul McCartney, George Harrison and Ringo Starr

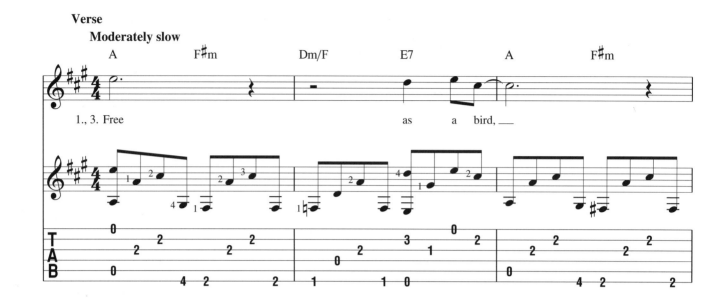

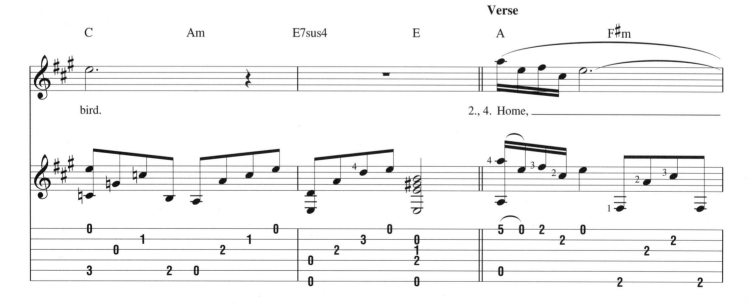

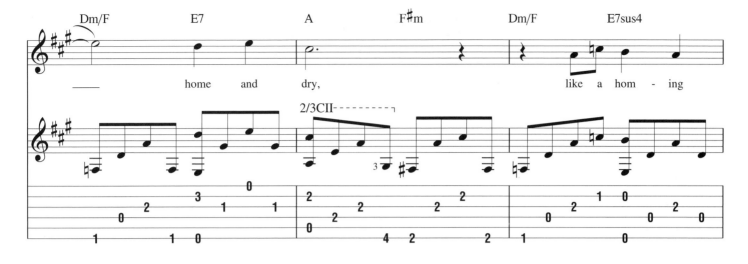

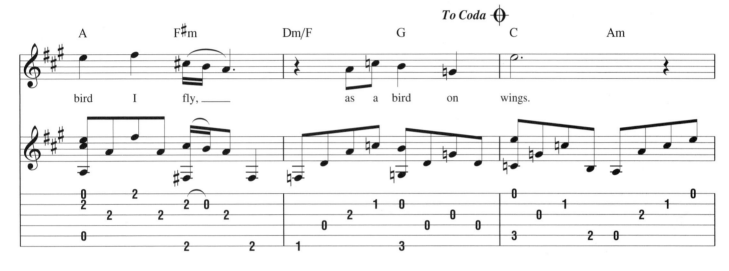

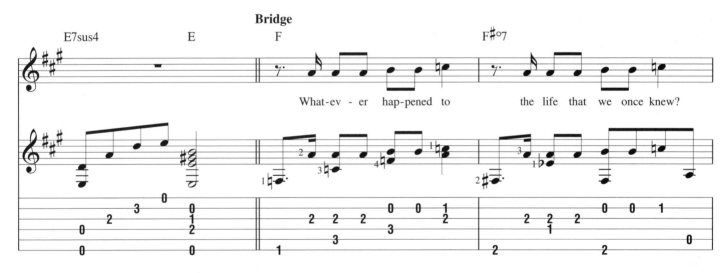

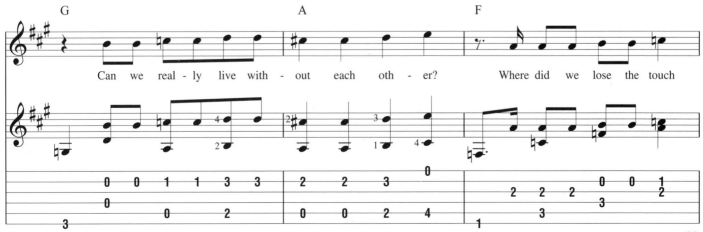

Coda

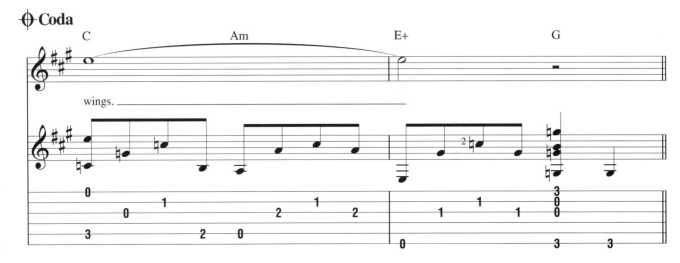

wings.

Bridge

Whatev - er hap-pened to the life that we once knew? Al - ways made me feel

Interlude

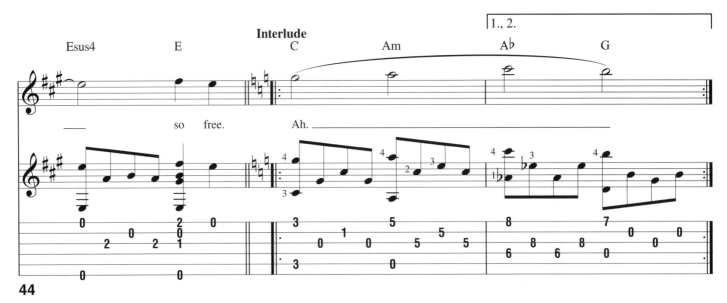

so free. Ah.

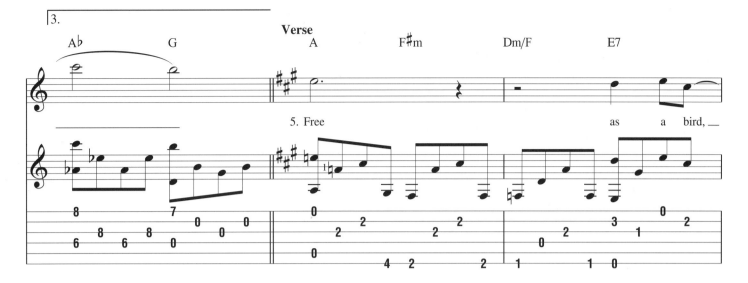

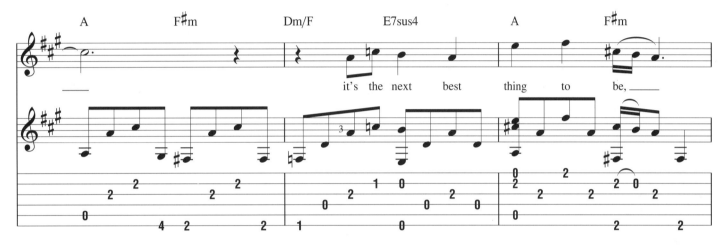

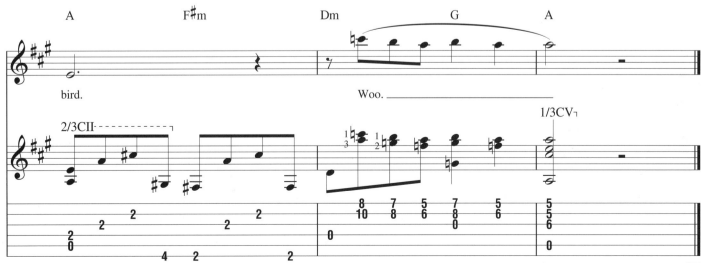

Hey Jude

Words and Music by John Lennon and Paul McCartney

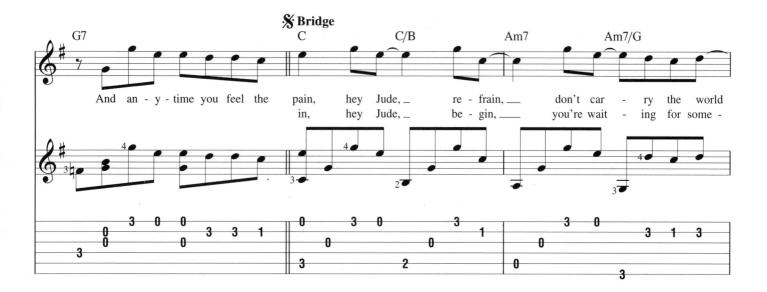

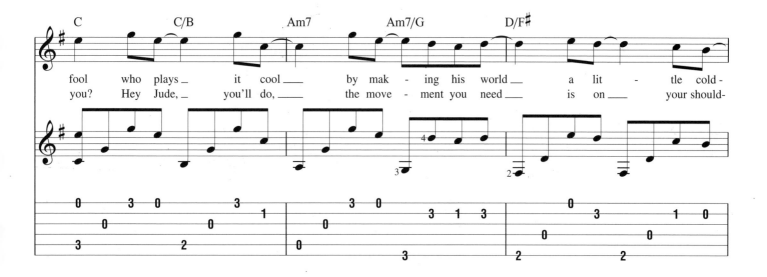

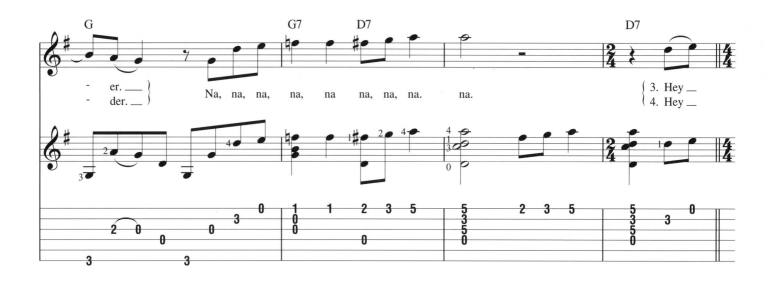

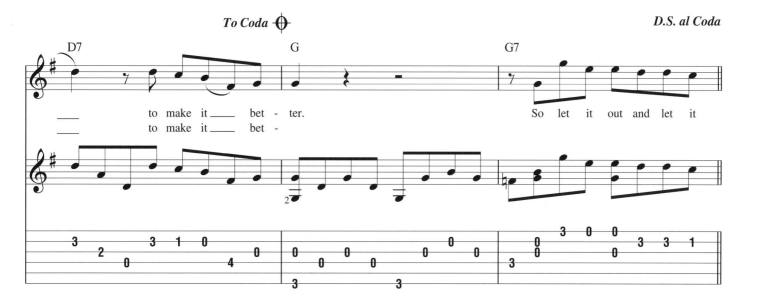

⊕ **Coda**

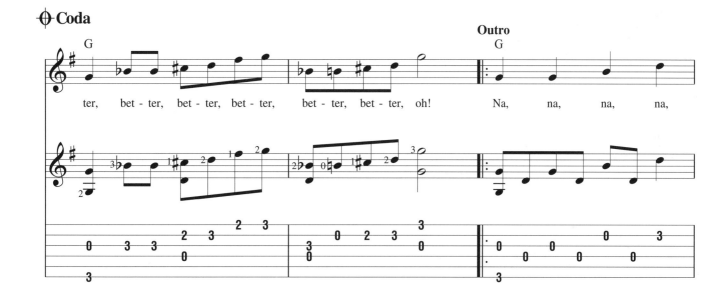

Repeat and fade

In My Life

Words and Music by John Lennon and Paul McCartney

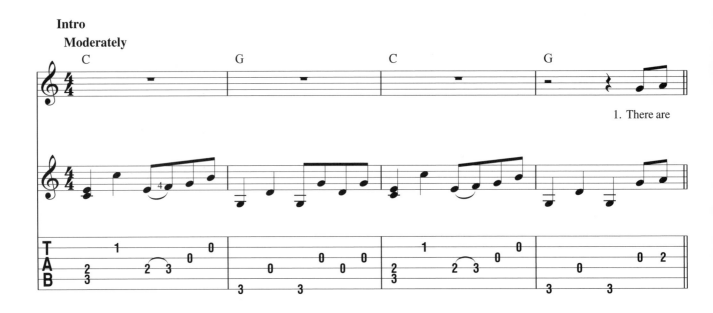

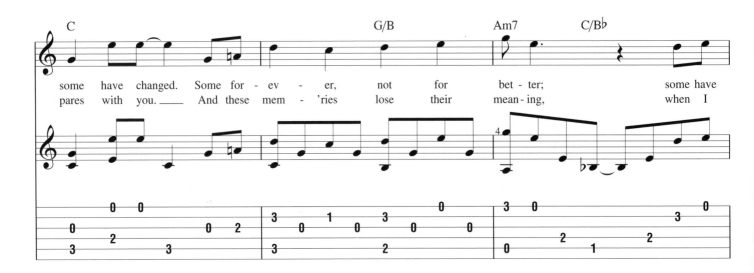

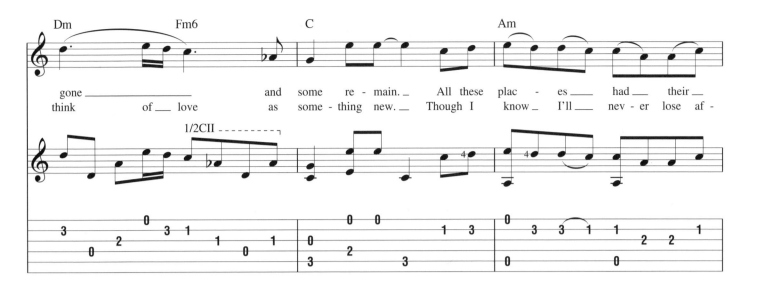

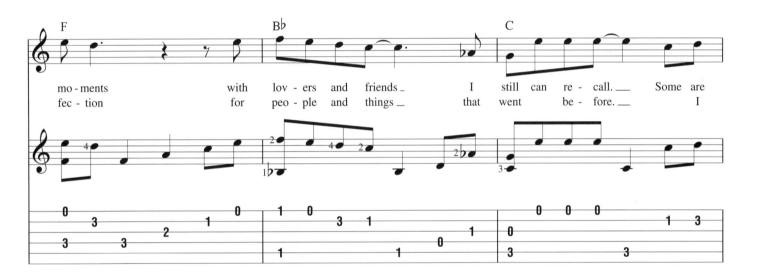

loved them all. ___

2. But of love you more. ___

Outro

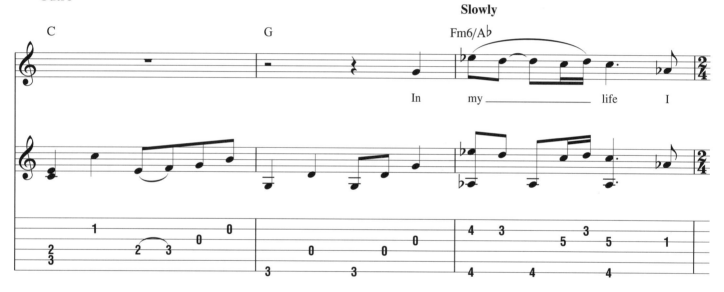

In my ___ life I

A tempo

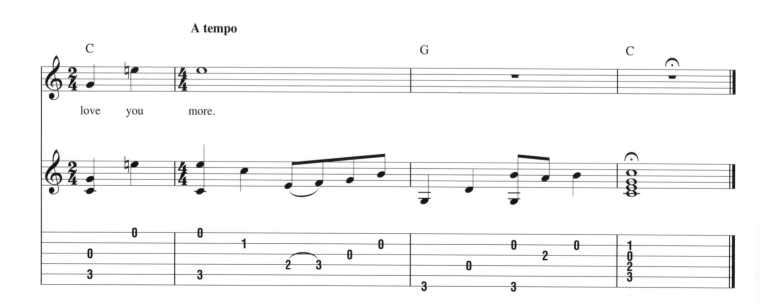

love you more.

Lady Madonna

Words and Music by John Lennon and Paul McCartney

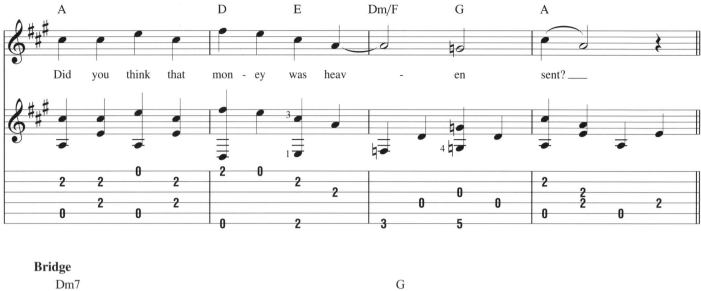

Did you think that mon-ey was heav — en sent? ___

Bridge

1. Fri - day night ___ ar - rives with - out a suit - case.
2. *Instrumental*
3. *See additional lyrics*

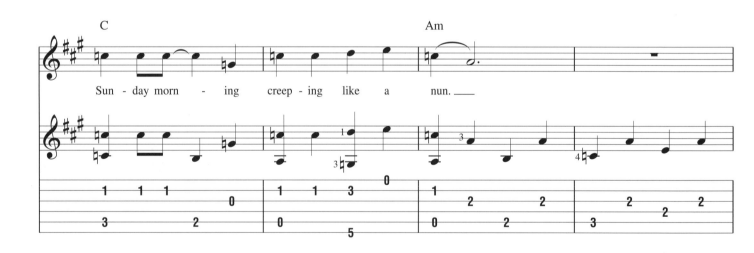

Sun - day morn — ing creep - ing like a nun. ___

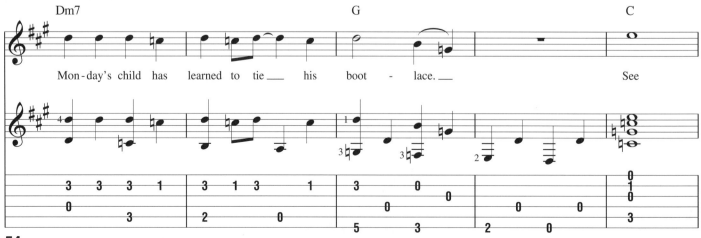

Mon - day's child has learned to tie ___ his boot - lace. ___ See

54

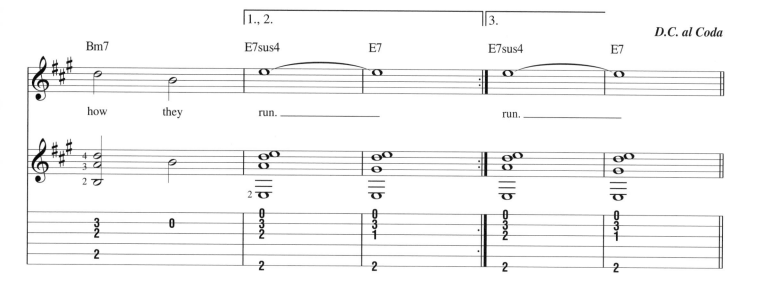

⊕ Coda

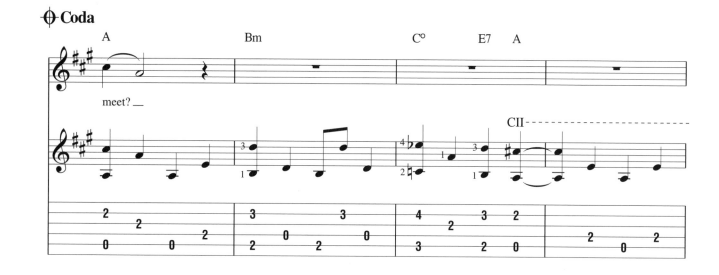

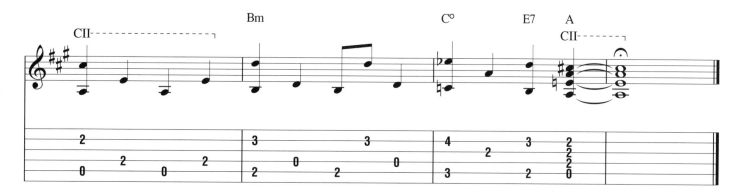

Additional Lyrics

2. Lady Madonna, baby at your breast,
   Wonders how you manage to feed the rest.

3. Lady Madonna, lying on the bed,
   Listen to the music playing in your head.

Bridge 3. Tuesday afternoon is never ending.
   Wednesday morning papers didn't come.
   Thursday night your stockings needed mending.
   See how they run.

Let It Be

Words and Music by John Lennon and Paul McCartney

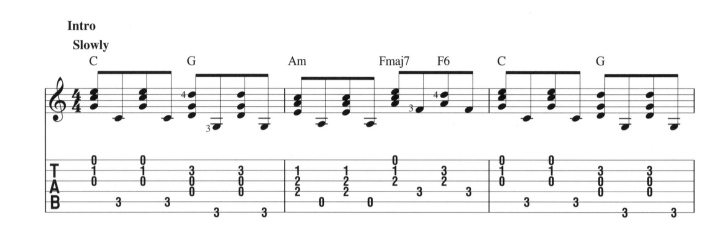

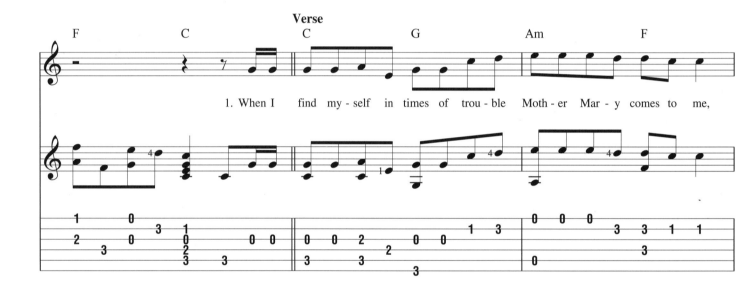

stand-ing right in front of me, speak-ing words of wis-dom, __ let it be. __ Let it

Chorus

be, let it be, __ let it be, __ let it be. Whis-per words of wis-dom, __ let it

Verse

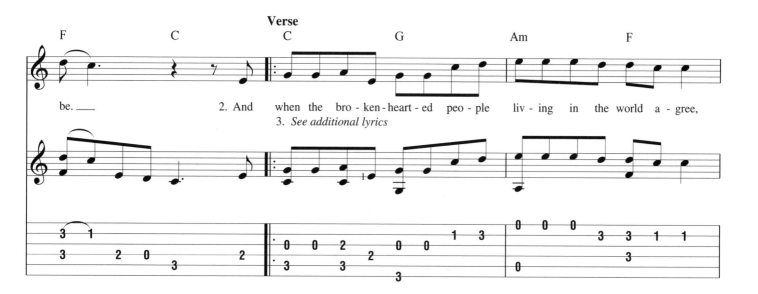

be. __ 2. And when the bro-ken-heart-ed peo-ple liv-ing in the world a-gree,
3. *See additional lyrics*

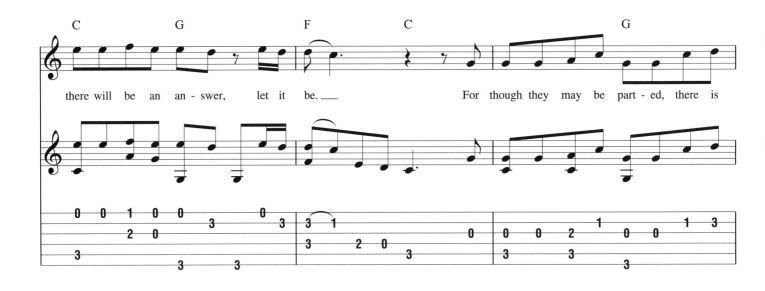

there will be an an - swer, let it be. ___ For though they may be part - ed, there is

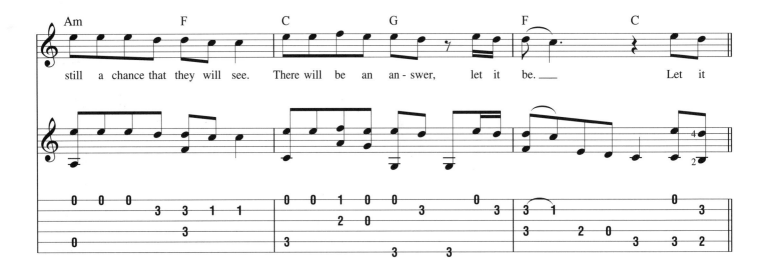

still a chance that they will see. There will be an an - swer, let it be. ___ Let it

Chorus

be, let it be, ___ let it be, ___ let it be. There will be an an - swer, let it

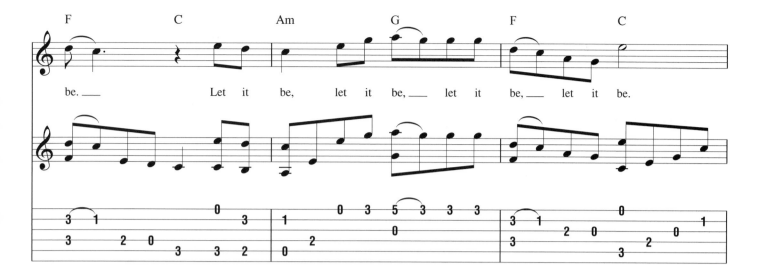

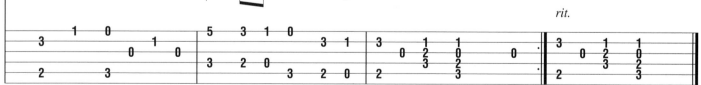

Additional Lyrics

3. And when the night is cloudy, there is still a light that shines on me,
   Shine until tomorrow, let it be.
   I wake up to the sound of music, Mother Mary comes to me,
   Speaking words of wisdom, let it be.

The Long and Winding Road

Words and Music by John Lennon and Paul McCartney

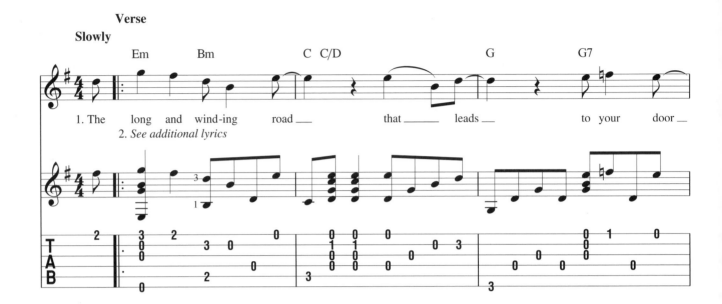

1. The long and wind-ing road ___ that ___ leads ___ to your door ___
2. *See additional lyrics*

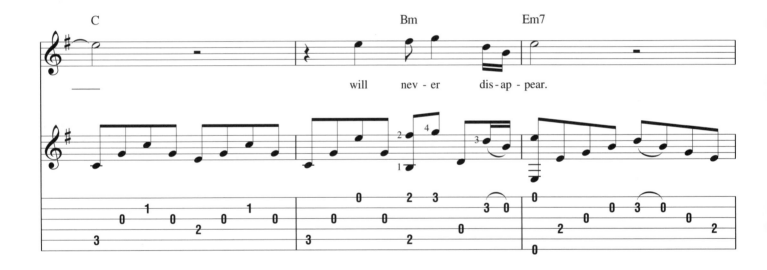

___ will nev-er dis-ap-pear.

I've seen that road be-fore. ___ It al-ways leads ___

_____ me here. Lead me to your _ door. 2. The

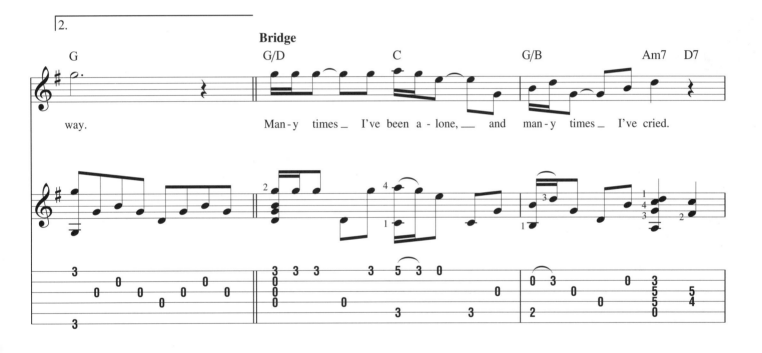

way. **Bridge** Man-y times _ I've been a - lone, _ and man-y times _ I've cried.

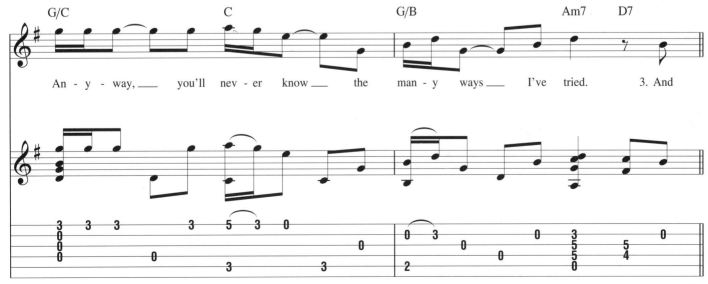

An - y - way, _ you'll nev - er know _ the man - y ways _ I've tried. 3. And

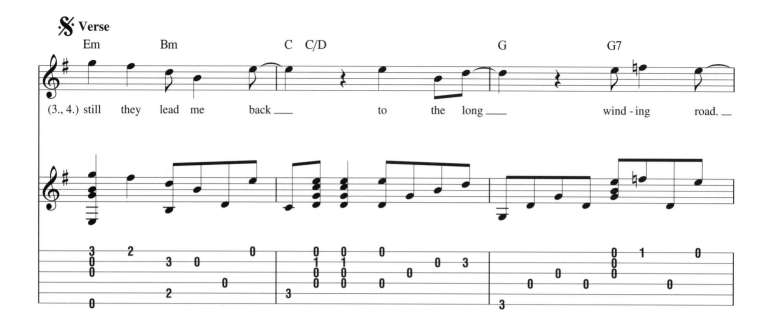

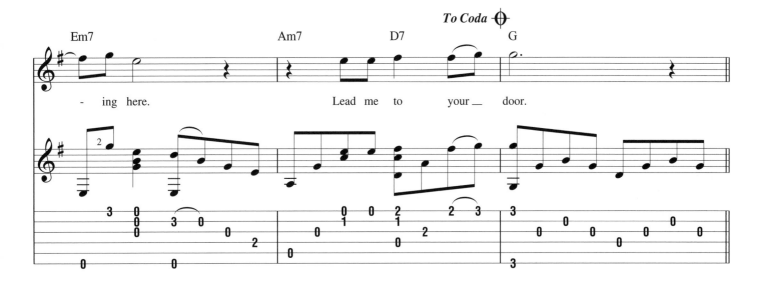

D.S. al Coda

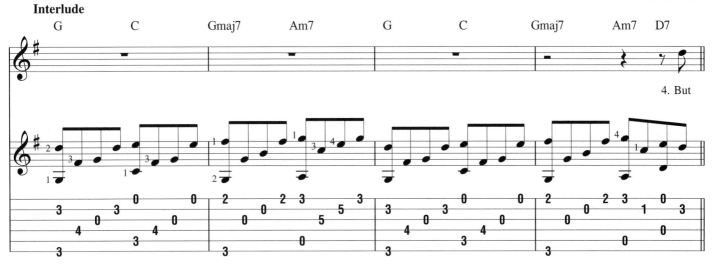

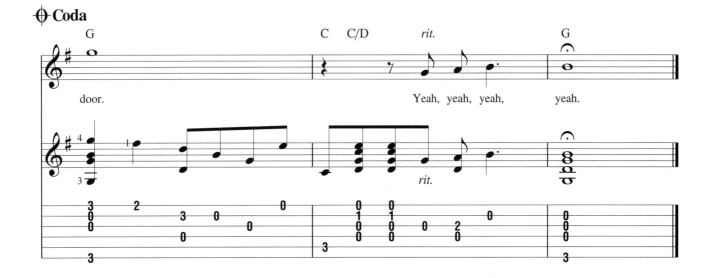

Additional Lyrics

2. The wild and windy night
   That the rain washed away
   Has left a pool of tears
   Crying for the day.
   Why leave me standing here?
   Let me know the way.

Love Me Do

Words and Music by John Lennon and Paul McCartney

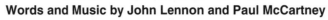

Intro
Moderately

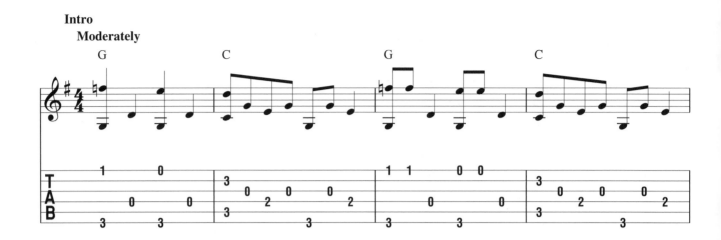

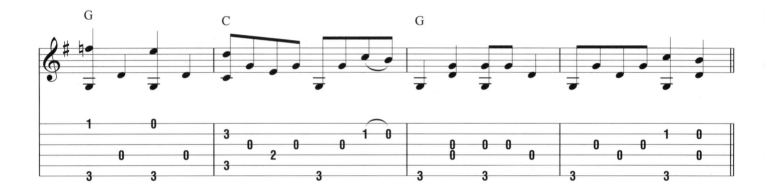

Verse

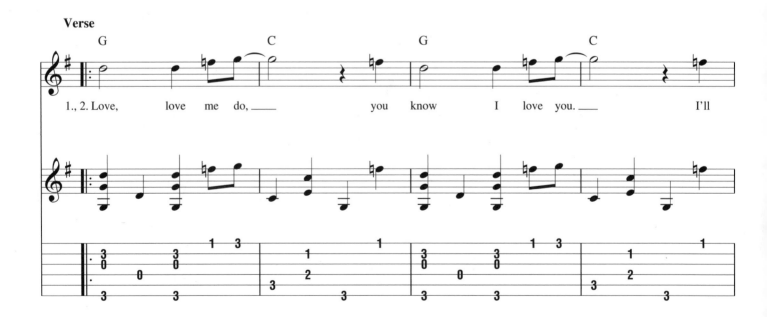

1., 2. Love, love me do, ___ you know I love you. ___ I'll

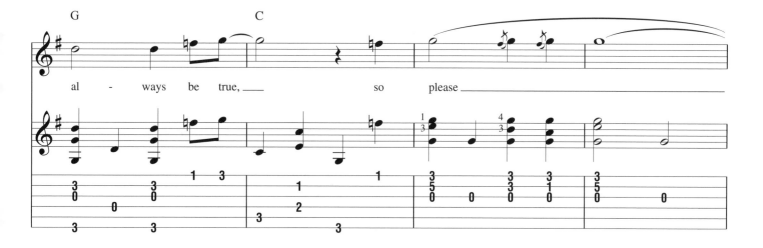

al - ways be true, ___ so please ___

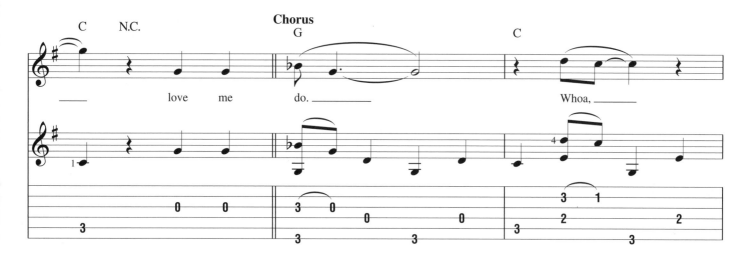

___ love me do. ___ Whoa, ___

Chorus

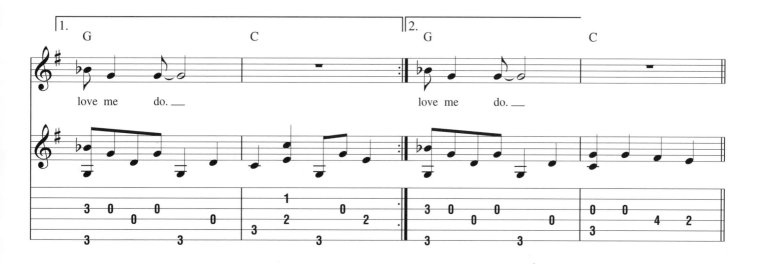

love me do. ___ love me do. ___

Bridge

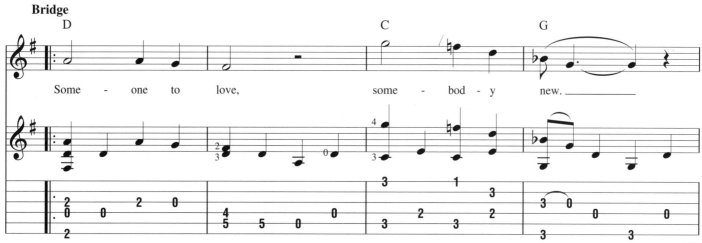

Some - one to love, some - bod - y new. ___

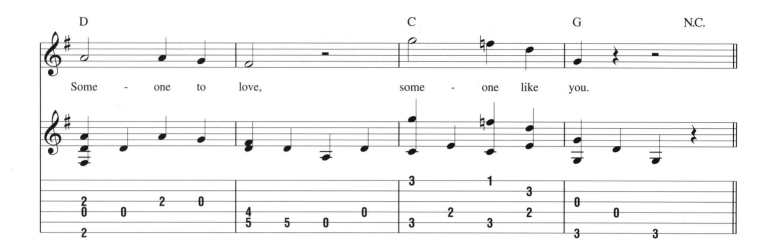

Some - one to love, some - one like you.

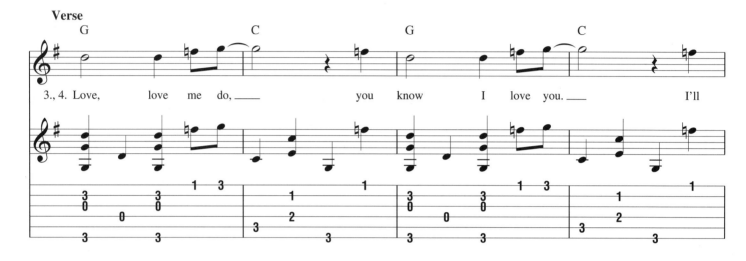

Verse

3., 4. Love, love me do, ___ you know I love you. ___ I'll

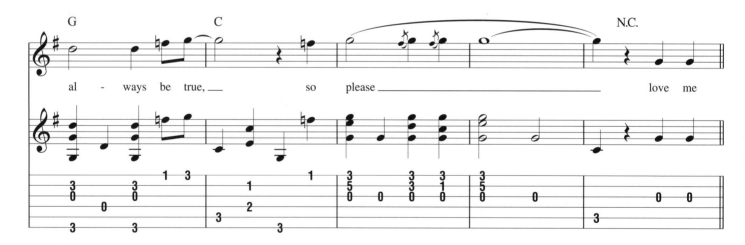

al - ways be true, ___ so please _____ love me

Chorus

do. ___ Whoa, ___ love me do. ___

Nowhere Man

Words and Music by John Lennon and Paul McCartney

Is - n't he ___ a bit like you ___ and me? ___ 1., 3. No - where
No - where man ___ can you see me ___ at all? ___ 2. No - where

Chorus

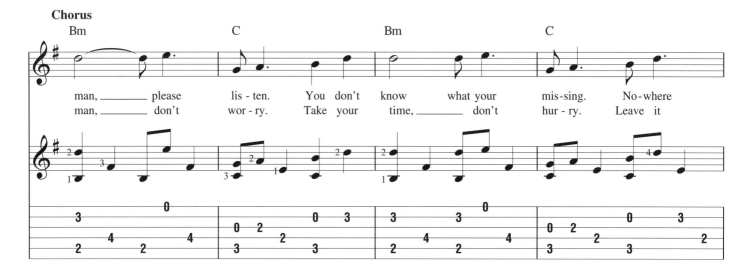

man, ___ please lis - ten. You don't know what your mis - sing. No - where
man, ___ don't wor - ry. Take your time, ___ don't hur - ry. Leave it

To Coda 1 ⊕   *To Coda 2* ⊕

man, the world ___ is at your com - mand.
all 'til some - bod - y else ___ lends you a hand.

Guitar Solo

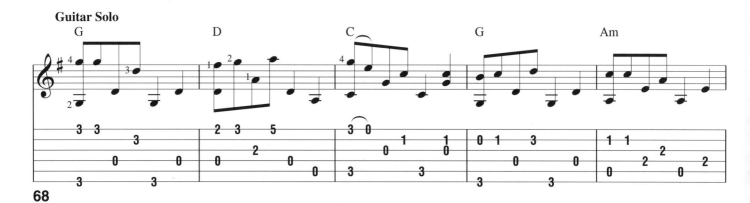

68

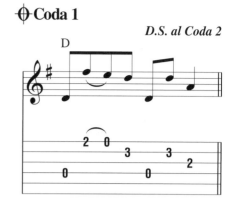

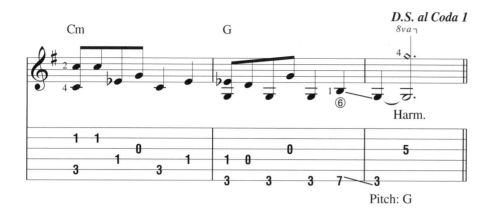

Pitch: G

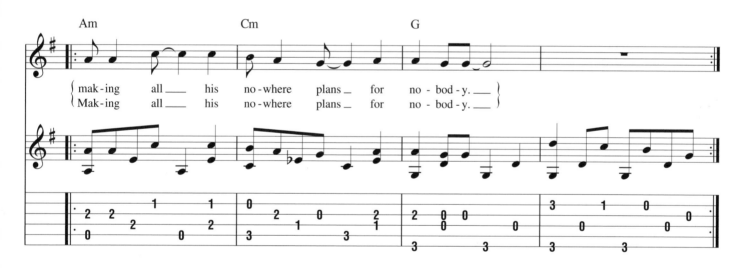

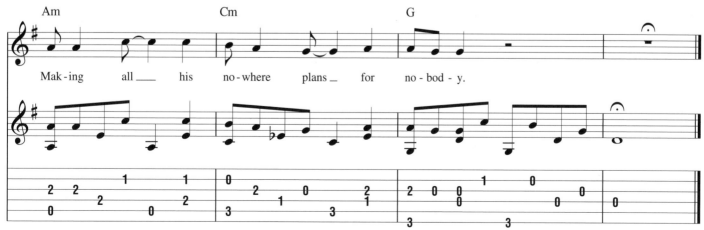

Michelle

Words and Music by John Lennon and Paul McCartney

semble, tres bien en - semble.

1. I love you, I love you, I love you,
2. I need to, I need to, I need to,

that's all I want to say.
I need to make you see,

Un - til I find a way, ___
oh, what you mean to me. ___

I will
Un -

say the on - ly words I know that you'll un - der - stand.
til I do, I'm hop - ing you will know what I

mean.

Guitar Solo

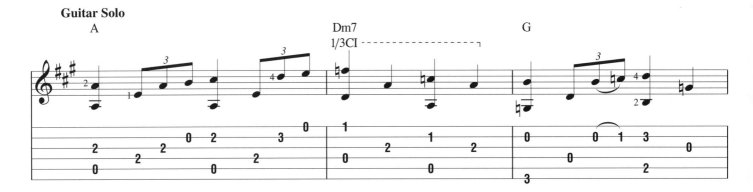

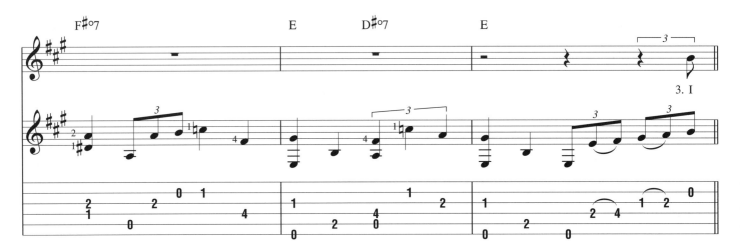

Verse

want you, I want you, I want you, I think you know by now,

I'll get to you some - how. Un - til I do, I'm tell - ing you so

Chorus

you'll un - der - stand.   Mi - chelle,   ma belle,   sont des mots qui

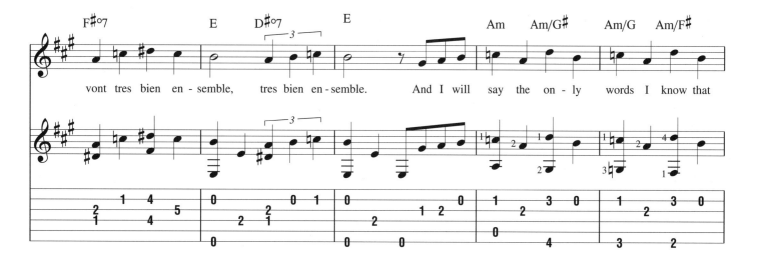

vont tres bien en - semble,   tres bien en - semble.   And I will   say   the on - ly   words I know that

Outro

you'll un - der - stand,   my Mi - chelle.

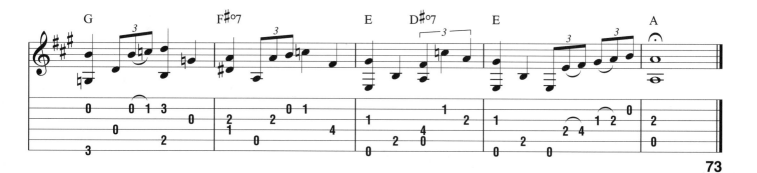

Norwegian Wood
(This Bird Has Flown)
Words and Music by John Lennon and Paul McCartney

Drop D tuning:
(low to high) D-A-D-G-B-E

Verse
Moderately

1. I once had a girl, or should I say she once had me.
3. *Instrumental*

She showed me her room, is-n't it good, Nor-we-gian wood. She
She

Bridge

asked me to stay, and she told me to sit an-y-where, So,
told me she worked in the morn-ing and start-ed to laugh. I

Ob-La-Di, Ob-La-Da

Words and Music by John Lennon and Paul McCartney

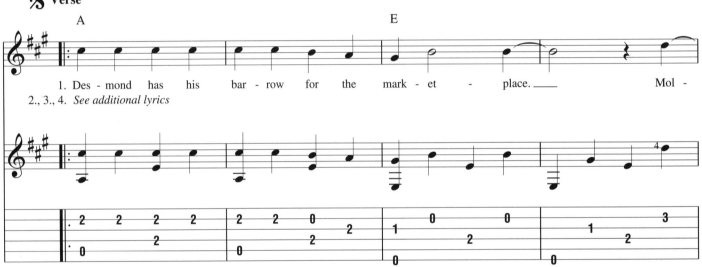

-mond says to Mol - ly, "Girl I like your face," ___ and Mol - ly

says this as she takes him by the hand. Ob - la - di,

Chorus

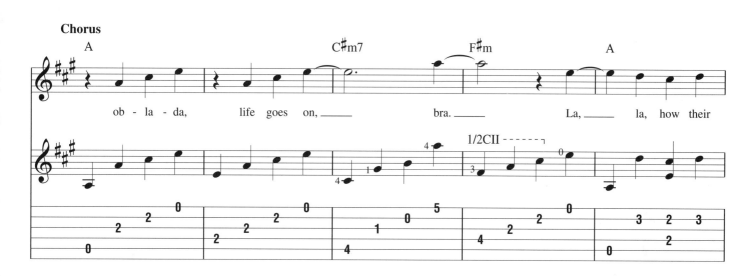

ob - la - da, life goes on, ___ bra. ___ La, ___ la, how their

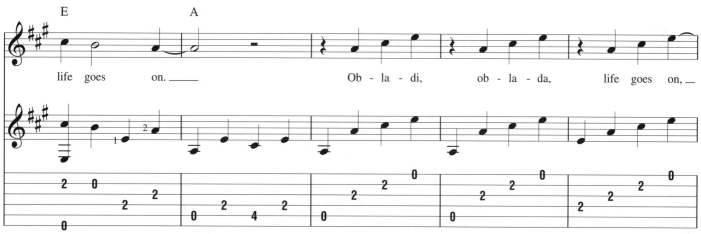

life goes on. ___ Ob - la - di, ob - la - da, life goes on, __

4th time, to Coda ⊕

C#m7   F#m   A   E   A

bra. ___   La, ___ la, how their life goes on. ___

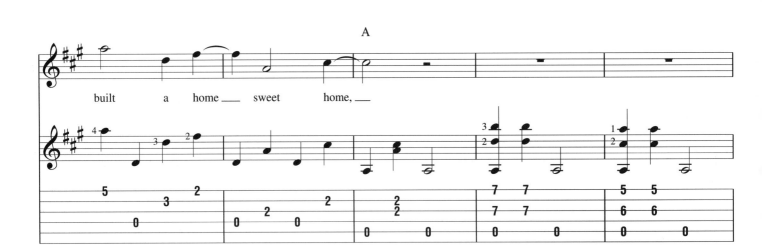

1.   2.   **Bridge**

D

In a cou-ple of   years   they have

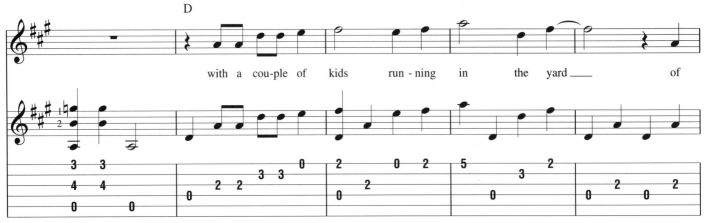

A

built   a home ___ sweet   home, ___

D

with a cou-ple of kids run-ning in the yard ___ of

78

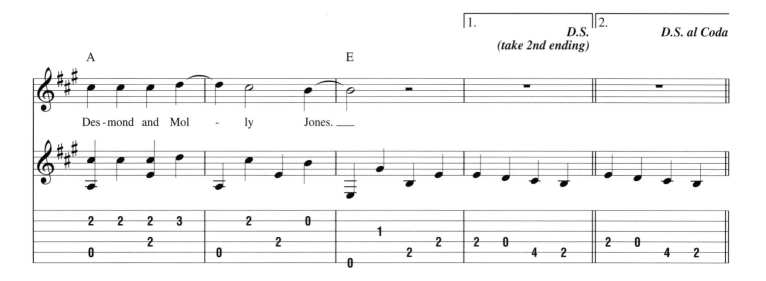

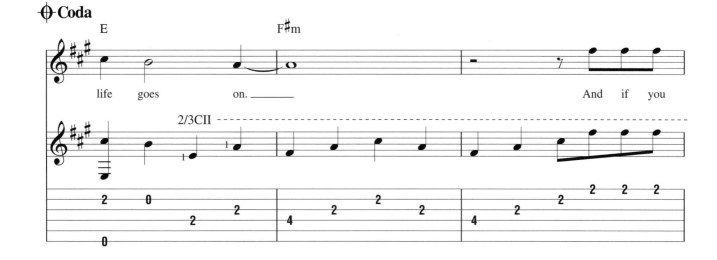

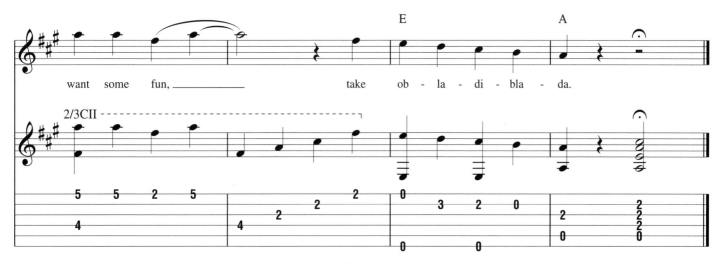

Additional Lyrics

2. Desmond takes a trolly to the jeweler's store,
   Buys a twenty karat golden ring.
   Takes it back to Molly waiting at the door,
   And as he gives it to her she begins to sing.

3. Happy ever after in the market place,
   Desmond lets the children lend a hand.
   Molly stays at home and does her pretty face
   And in the evening she still sings it with the band.

4. Happy ever after in the market place,
   Molly lets the children lend a hand.
   Desmond stays at home and does his pretty face
   And in the evening she's a singer with the band.

Octopus's Garden

Words and Music by Richard Starkey

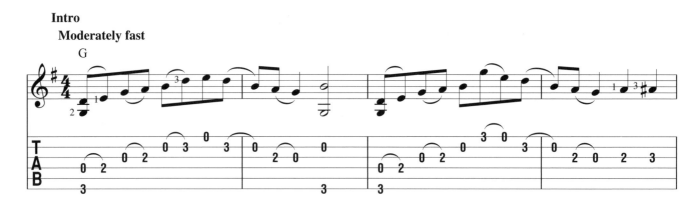

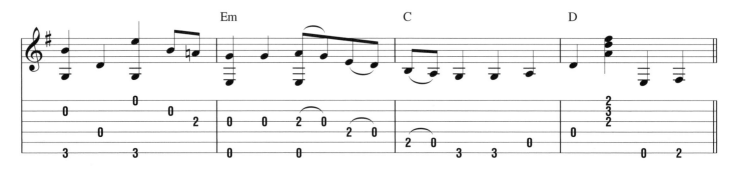

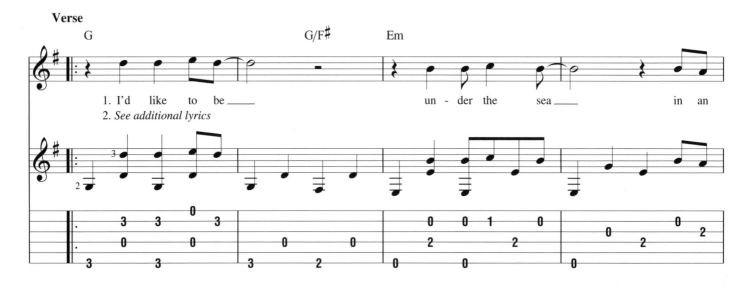

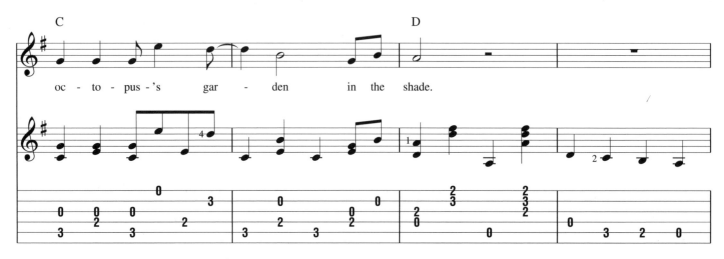

He'd let us in, ____ know where we've been, ___ in his

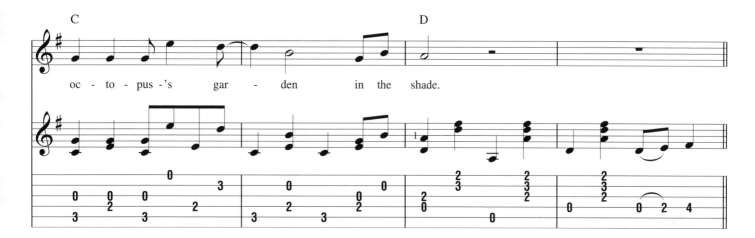

oc - to - pus -'s gar - den in the shade.

Pre-Chorus

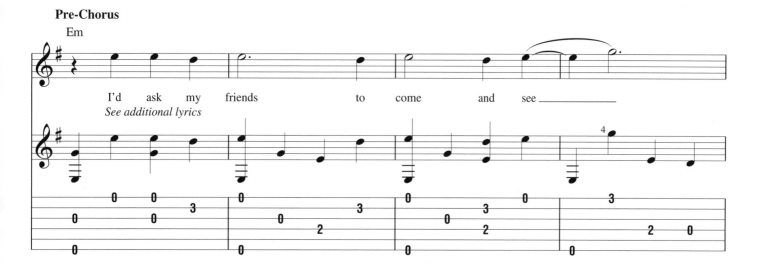

I'd ask my friends to come and see _____
See additional lyrics

an oc - to - pus -'s gar - den with me. _____

Chorus

I'd like to be _____ un - der the sea _____ in an

oc - to - pus -'s gar - den in the shade.

2.   **Interlude**

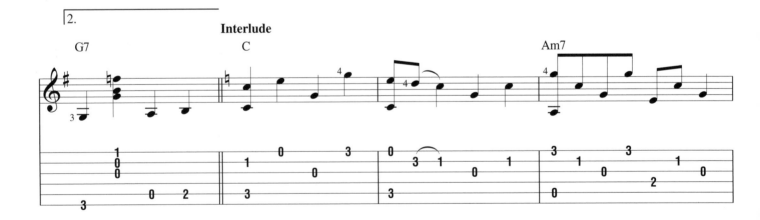

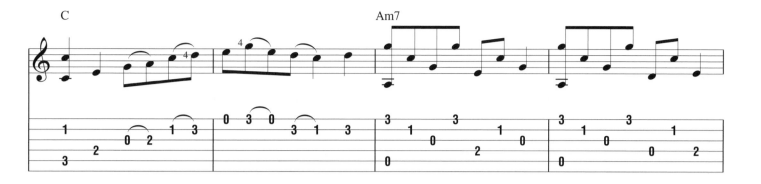

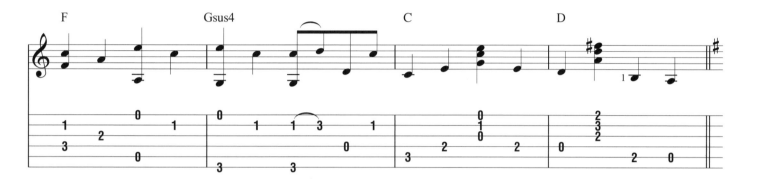

Verse

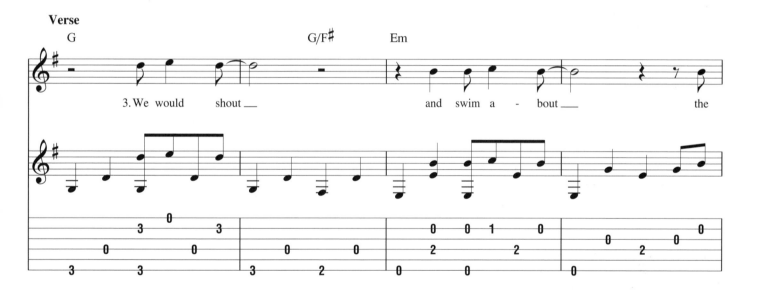

3. We would shout ___ and swim a - bout ___ the

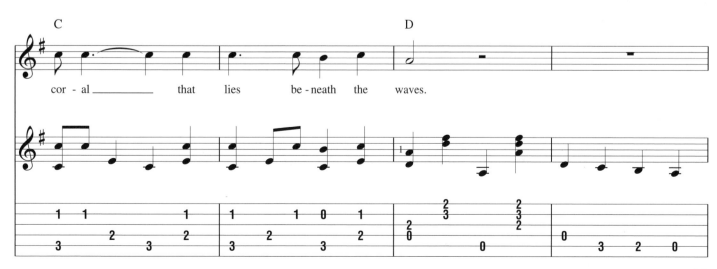

cor - al ___ that lies be - neath the waves.

Oh, what joy ___ for ev - 'ry girl and boy, ___

know - ing ___ they're hap - py and they're safe.

Pre-Chorus

We would be so hap - py you and me,

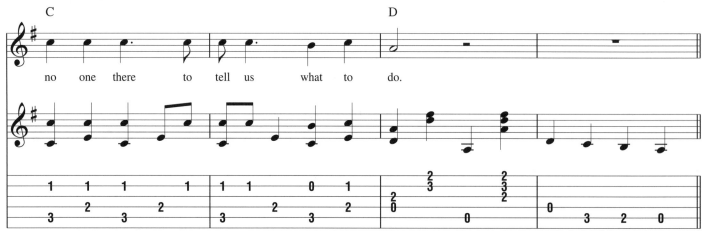

no one there to tell us what to do.

Chorus

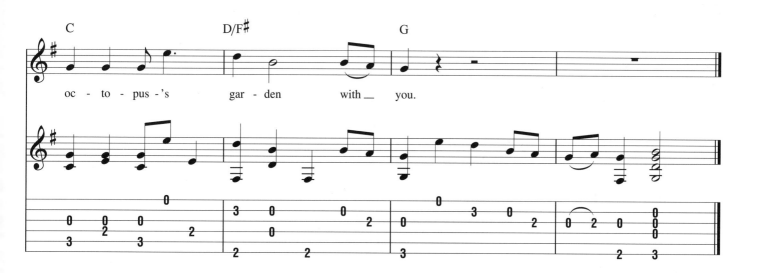

Additional Lyrics

2. We would be warm below the storm
   In our little hideaway beneath the waves.
   Resting our head on the sea bed
   In an octopus's garden near a cave.

Pre-Chorus We would sing and dance around
Because we know we can't be found.

Penny Lane

Words and Music by John Lennon and Paul McCartney

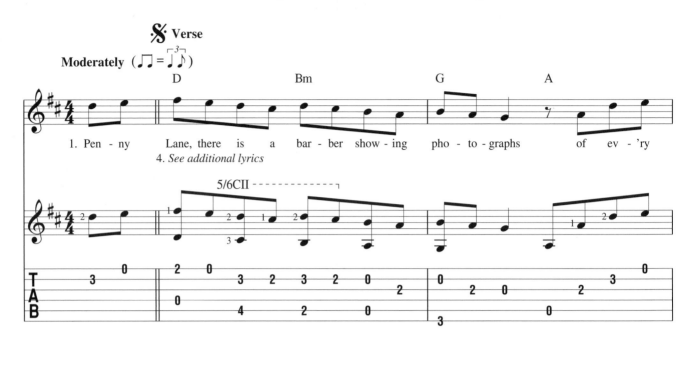

1. Pen - ny Lane, there is a bar - ber show - ing pho - to - graphs of ev - 'ry
4. *See additional lyrics*

head he's had the plea - sure to ___ know, ___ and all the peo - ple that come and go ___

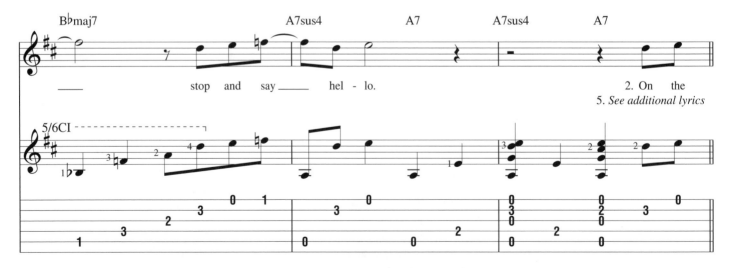

___ stop and say ___ hel - lo.

2. On the
5. *See additional lyrics*

*British slang for raincoat

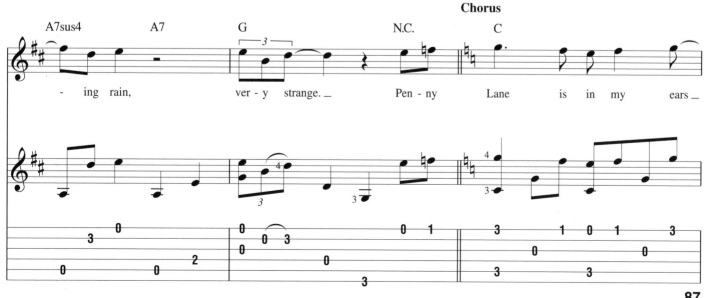

and in my eyes. ___

**T = Thumb on 6th string

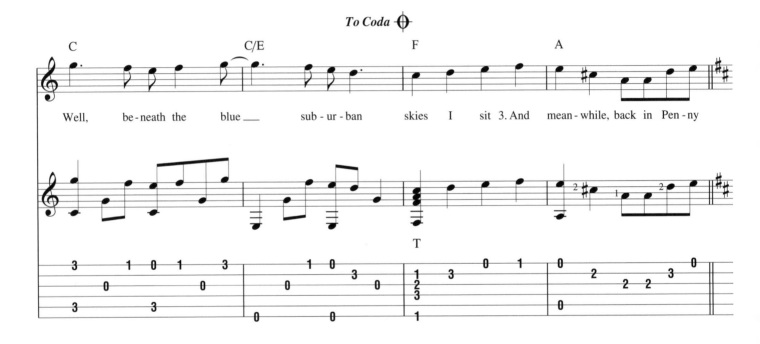

To Coda

Well, be-neath the blue ___ sub-ur-ban skies I sit 3. And mean-while, back in Pen-ny

Verse

Lane there is a fire-man with an hour ___ glass. And in his pock-et is a por-trait of the

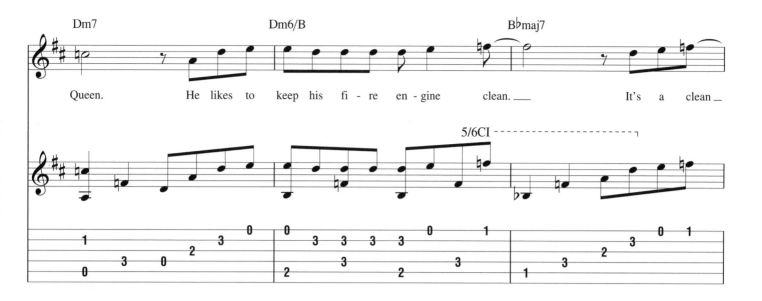

Queen. He likes to keep his fi - re en - gine clean. ___ It's a clean ___

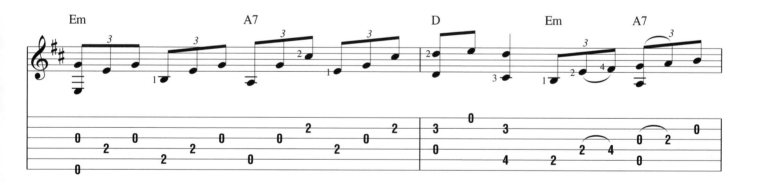

___ ma - chine.

Interlude

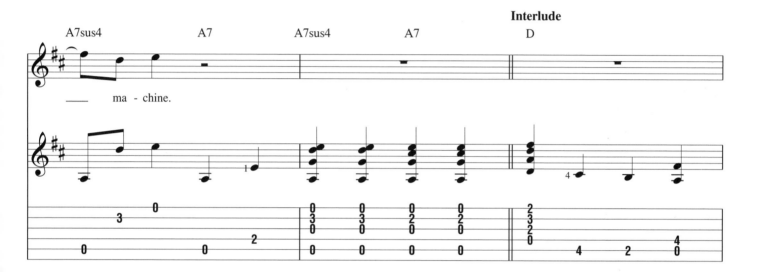

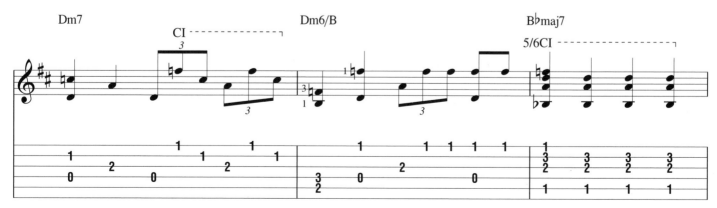

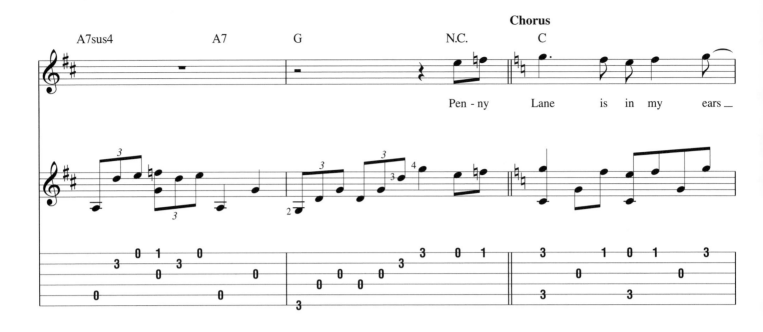

Chorus

A7sus4   A7   G   N.C.   C

Pen - ny   Lane   is   in   my   ears __

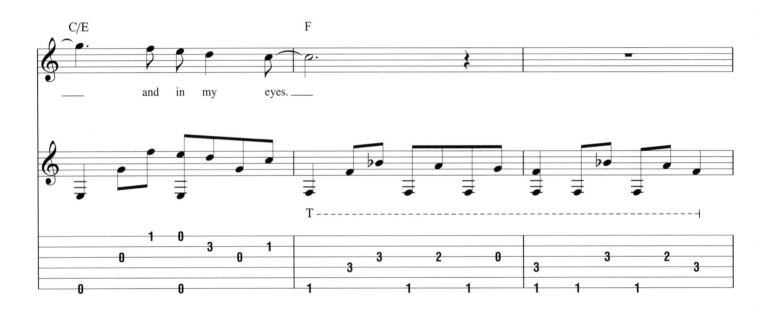

C/E   F

__   and   in   my   eyes. __

D.S. al Coda

C   F   A

Full   of   fish __   and   fin - ger   pies   in   sum - mer.   4. Mean - while,   back   be - hind   the

⊕ Coda

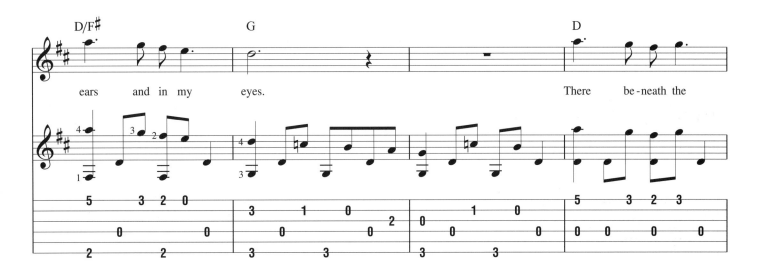

Additional Lyrics

4. Meanwhile, back behind the shelter in the middle of the roundabout,
   A pretty nurse is selling poppies from a tray.
   And though she feels as if she's in a play,
   She is anyway.

5. Penny Lane, the barber shaves another customer.
   We see the banker sitting, waiting for a trim.
   Then the fireman rushes in
   From the pouring rain, very strange.

Please Please Me

Words and Music by John Lennon and Paul McCartney

Drop D tuning:
(low to high) D-A-D-G-B-E

Intro

Moderately

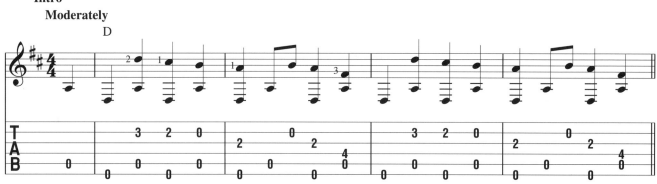

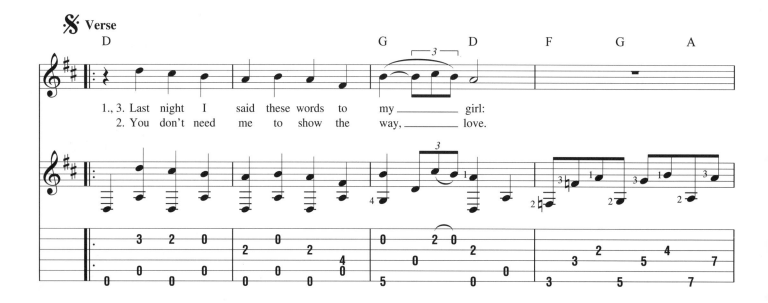

1., 3. Last night I said these words to my _____ girl:
2. You don't need me to show the way, _____ love.

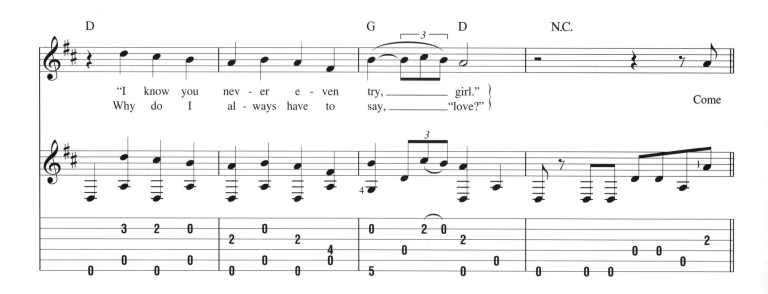

"I know you nev - er e - ven try, _____ girl."
Why do I al - ways have to say, _____ "love?"

Come

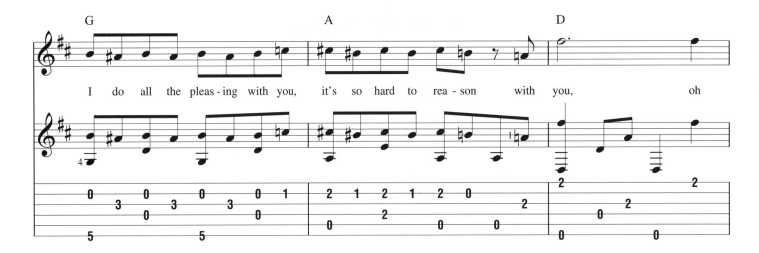

I do all the pleas-ing with you, it's so hard to rea-son with you, oh

D.S. al Coda

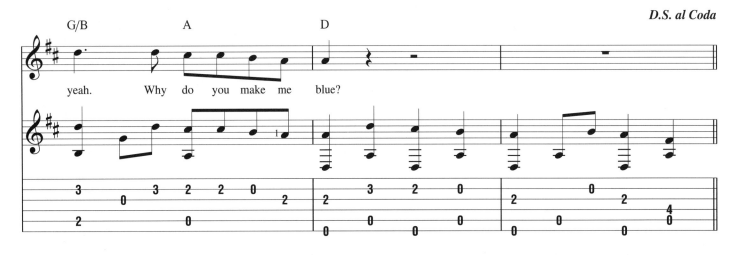

yeah. Why do you make me blue?

⊕ Coda

Outro

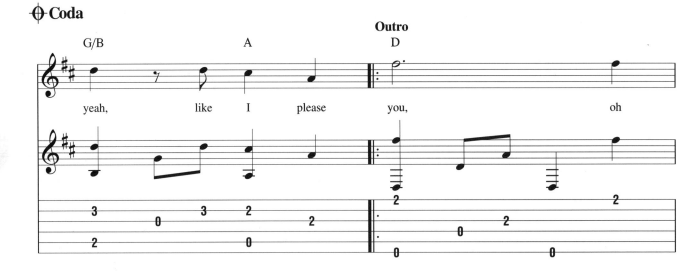

yeah, like I please you, oh

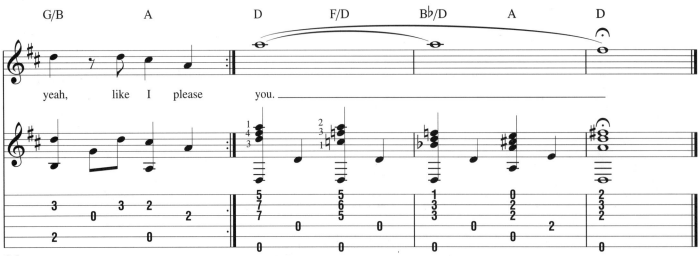

yeah, like I please you. _____

Something

Words and Music by George Harrison

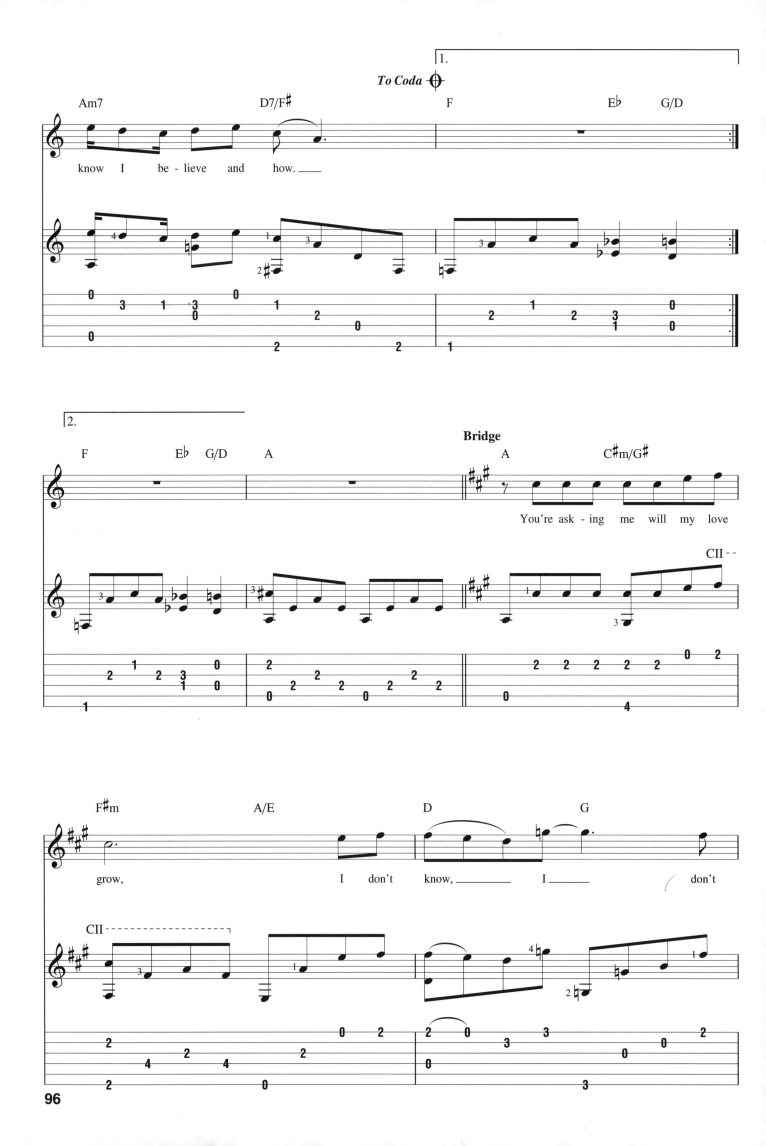

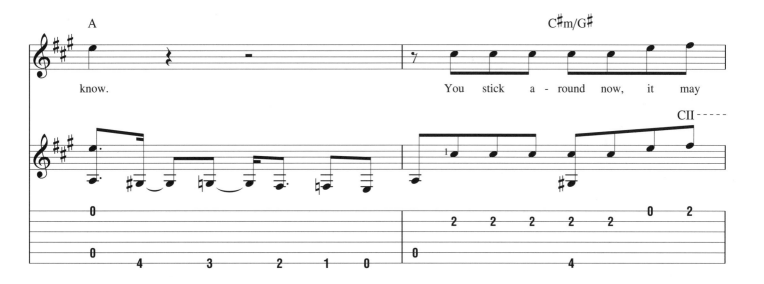

know.
You stick a - round now, it may

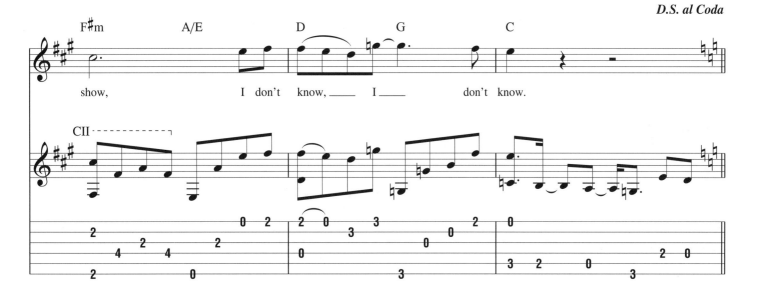

D.S. al Coda

show,
I don't know, ___ I ___ don't know.

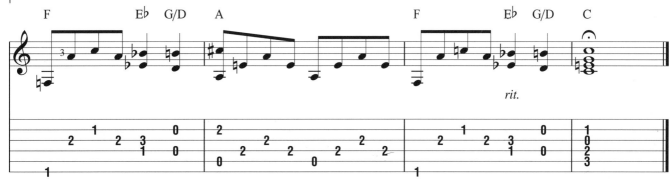

Coda

rit.

Additional Lyrics

2. Somewhere in her smile she knows
   That I don't need no other lover.
   Something in her style that shows me.
   I don't want to leave her now,
   You know I believe and how.

3. Something in the way she knows,
   And all I have to do is think of her.
   Something in the things she shows me.
   I don't want to leave her now,
   You know I believe and how.

Ticket to Ride

Words and Music by John Lennon and Paul McCartney

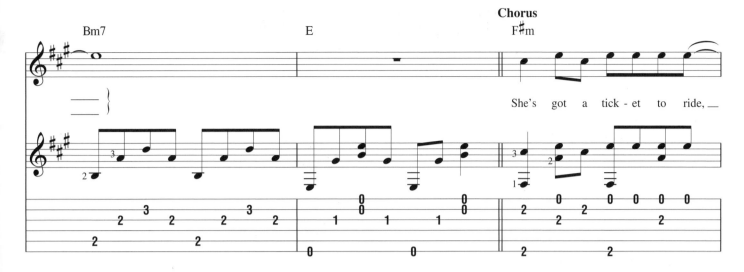

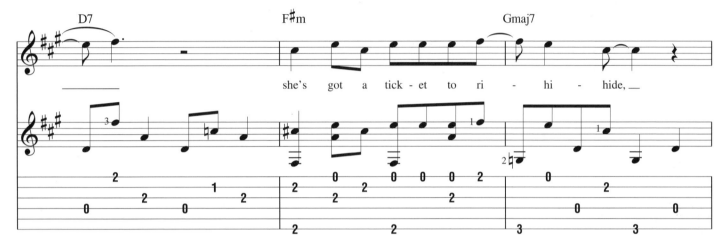

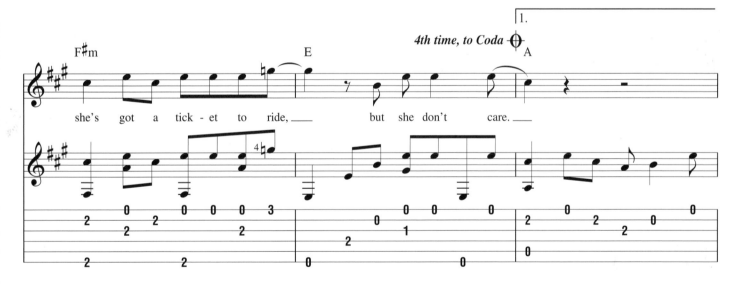

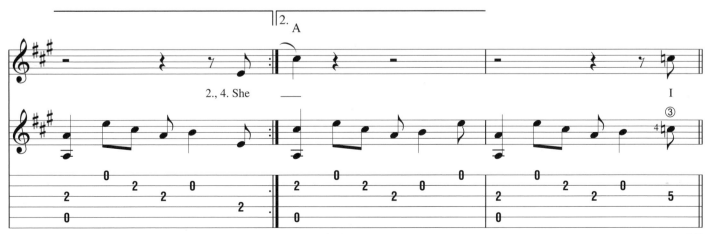

Bridge

don't know why she's rid-in' so high. _____ She ought-ta think twice, she ought-ta do right by

me. Be - fore she gets to say - in' good - bye, _____ she ought-ta

D.S. al Coda
(take repeat)

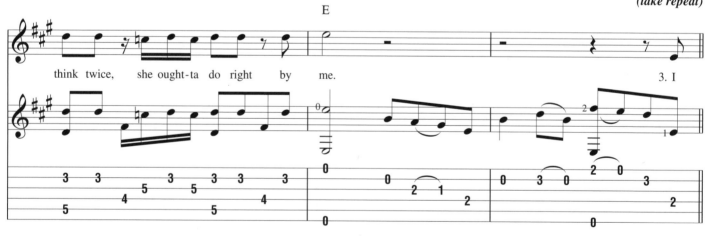

think twice, she ought-ta do right by me.

3. I

✦ **Coda**

Outro

My ba - by don't care.

We Can Work It Out

Words and Music by John Lennon and Paul McCartney

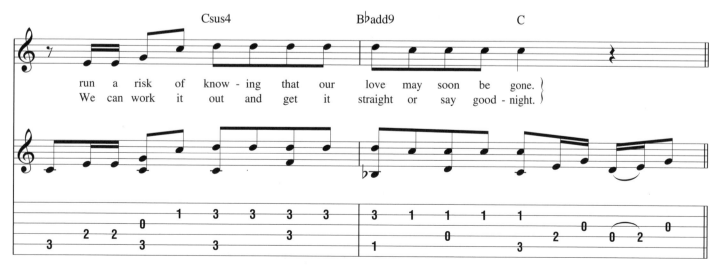

Chorus

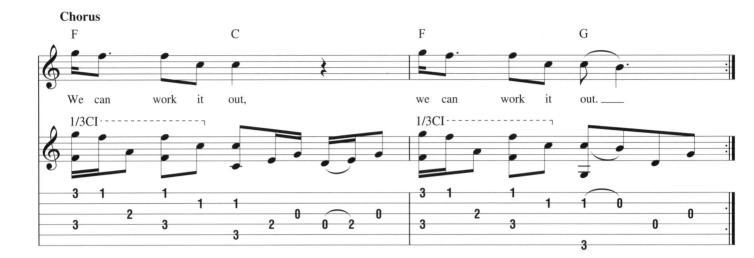

We can work it out, we can work it out.___

Bridge

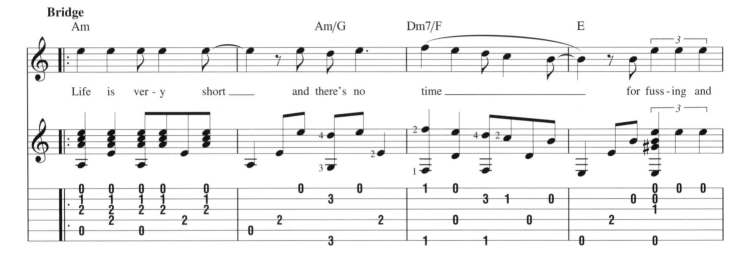

Life is ver-y short ___ and there's no time ___ for fuss-ing and

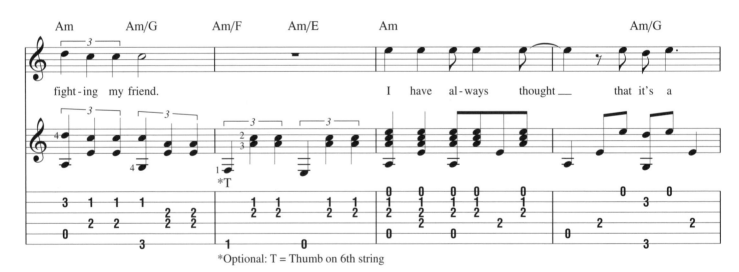

fight-ing my friend. I have al-ways thought ___ that it's a

*Optional: T = Thumb on 6th string

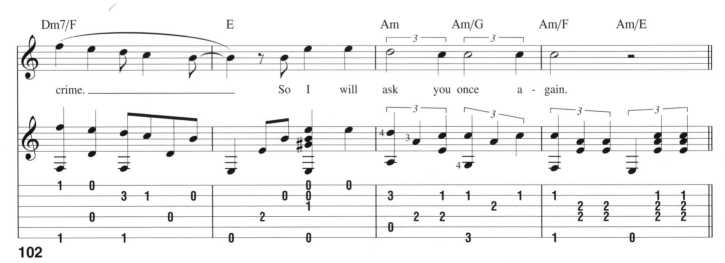

crime. ___ So I will ask you once a-gain.

Verse

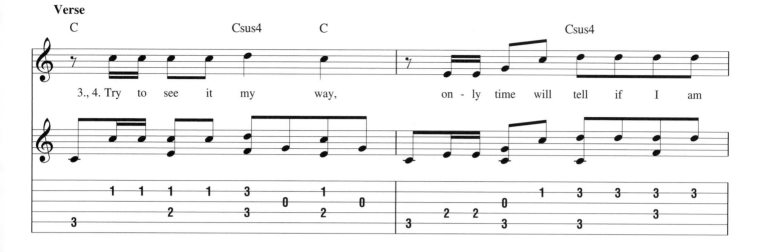

3., 4. Try to see it my way, on - ly time will tell if I am

right or I am wrong. While you see it your way,

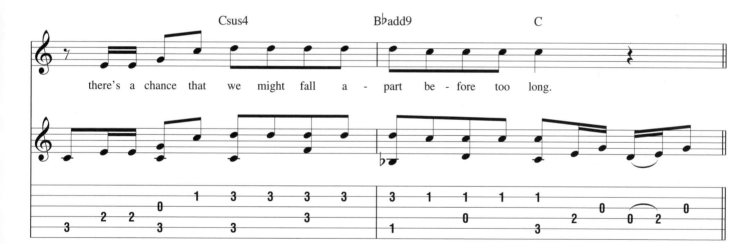

there's a chance that we might fall a - part be - fore too long.

Chorus   **Outro**

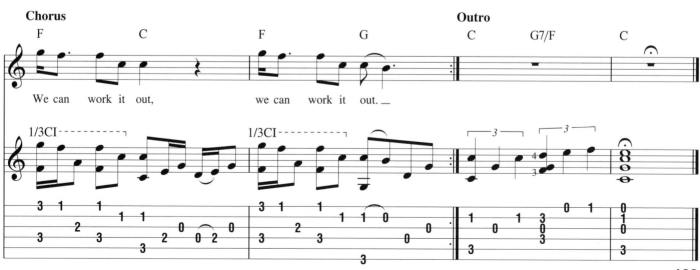

We can work it out, we can work it out.

When I'm Sixty Four

Words and Music by John Lennon and Paul McCartney

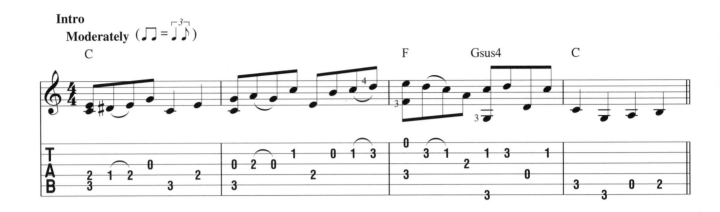

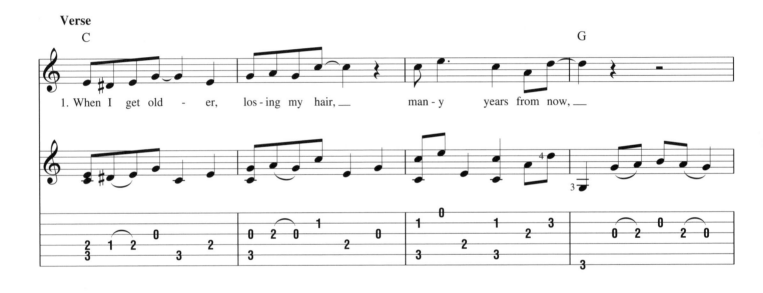

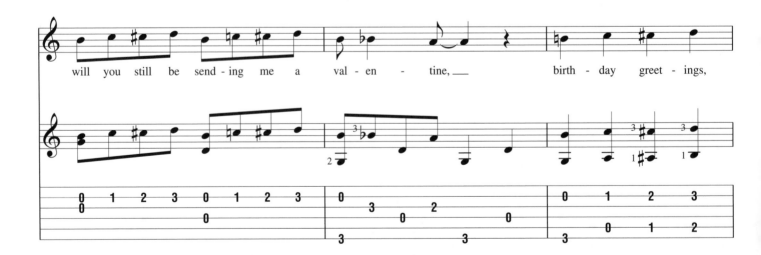

bot - tle of wine? __ If I'd been out __ till quar - ter to three, __

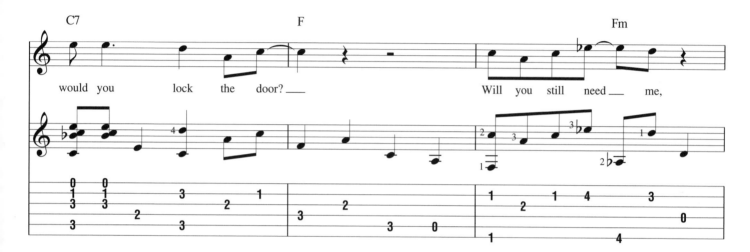

would you lock the door? __ Will you still need __ me,

will you still feed __ me when I'm six - ty - four?

Bridge

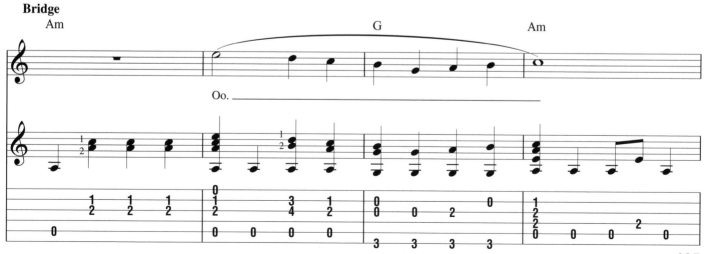

Oo. _____

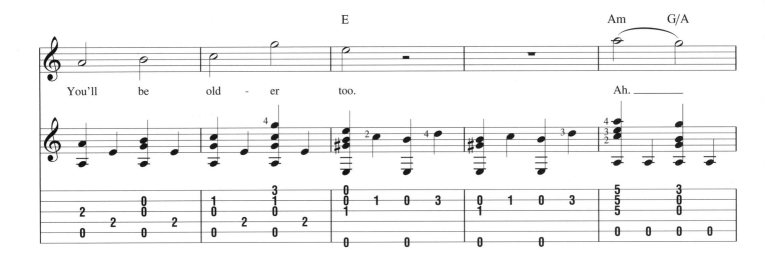

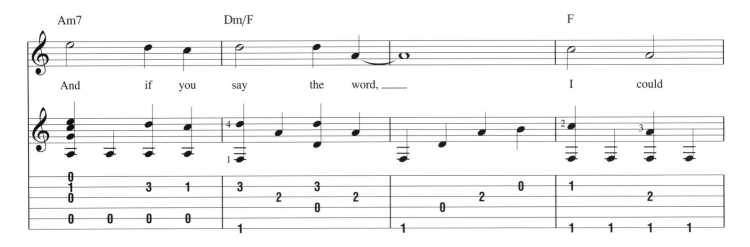

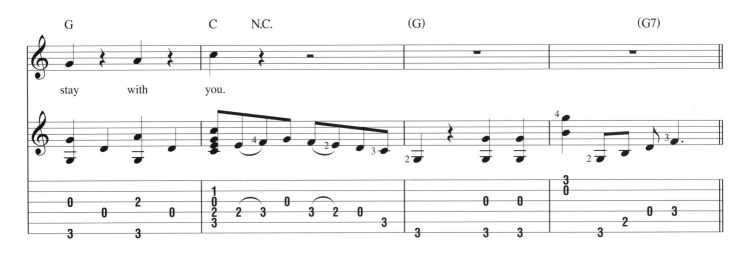

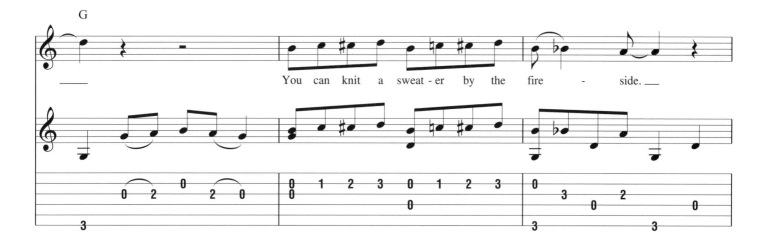

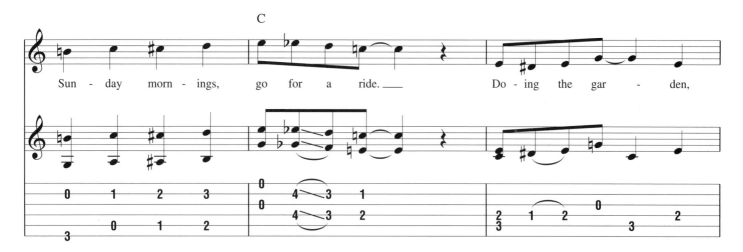

To Coda ⊕

Bridge

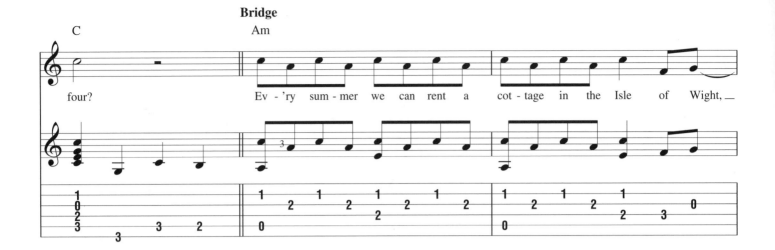

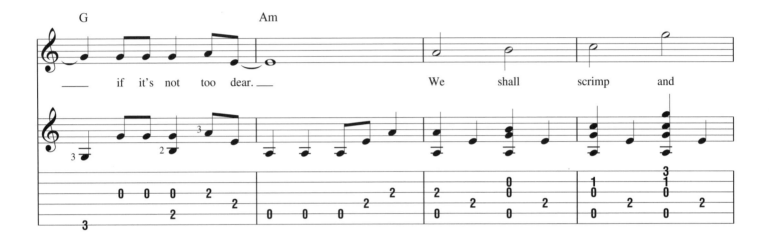

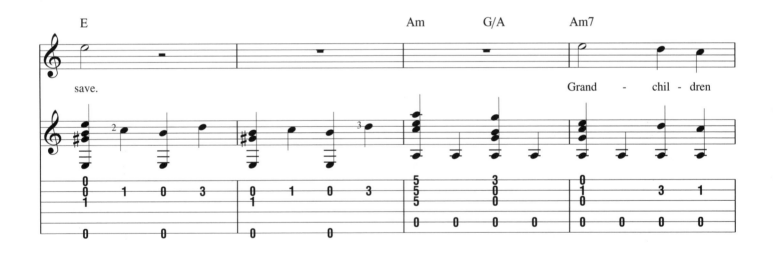

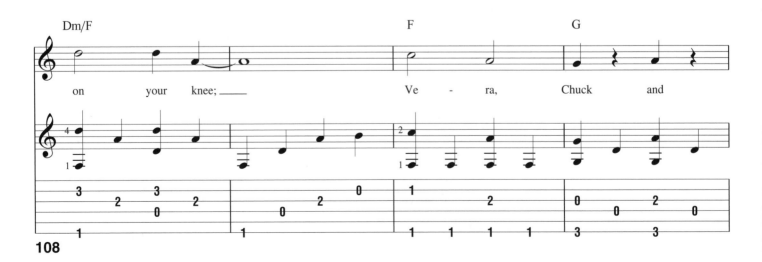

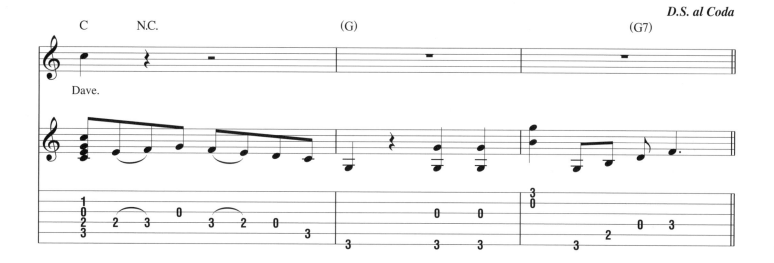

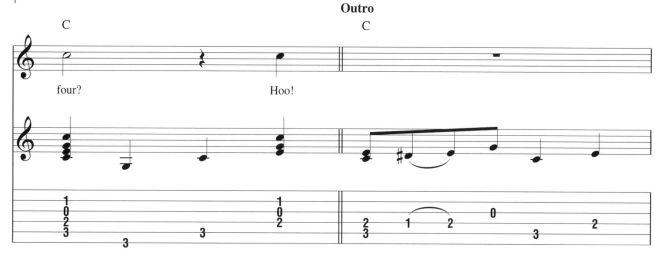

Coda

Outro

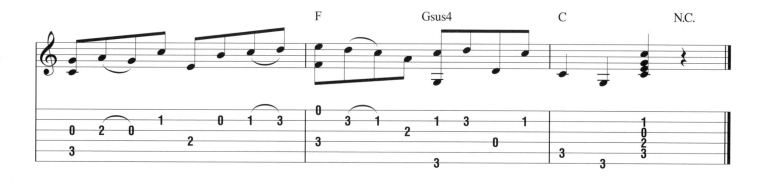

Additional Lyrics

3. Send me a postcard, drop me a line,
   Stating point of view.
   Indicate precisely what you mean to say.
   Yours sincerely wasting away.
   Give me your answer, fill in a form,
   Mine forevermore.
   Will you still need me, will you still feed me
   When I'm sixty-four?

Yellow Submarine

Words and Music by John Lennon and Paul McCartney

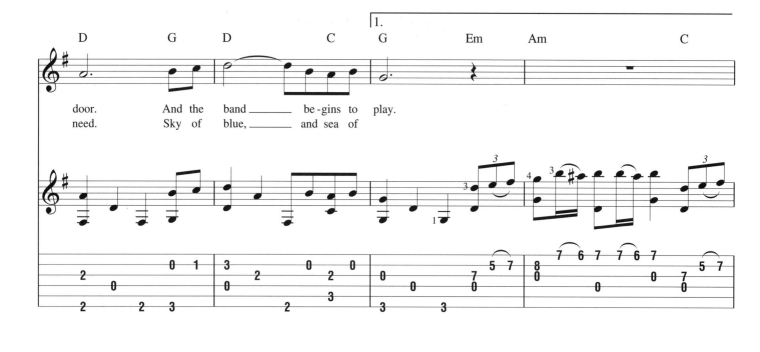

Outro-Chorus

Repeat and fade

Yesterday

Words and Music by John Lennon and Paul McCartney

Bridge

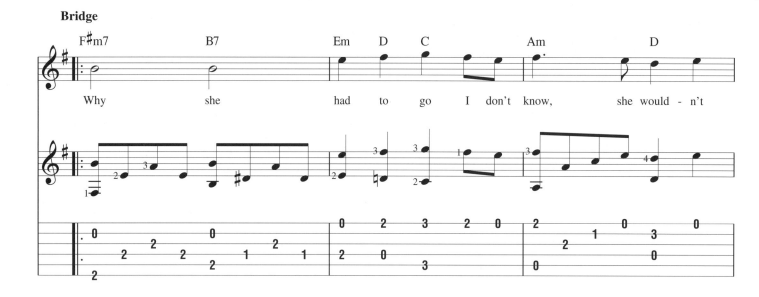

Why she had to go I don't know, she would-n't

say. I said some-thing wrong, now I

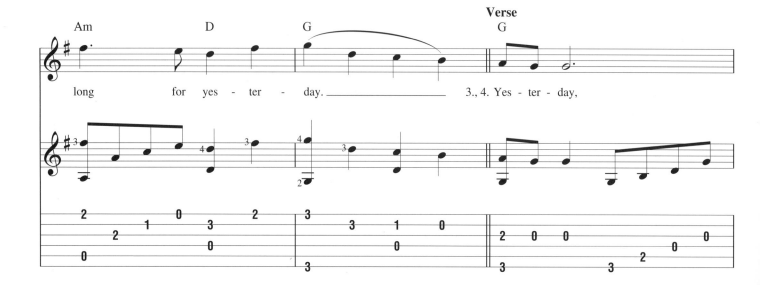

long for yes-ter-day. _____ 3., 4. Yes-ter-day,

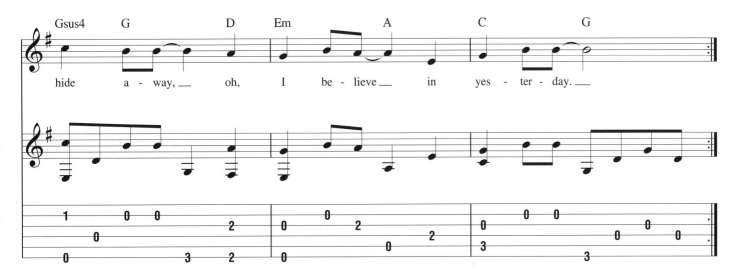

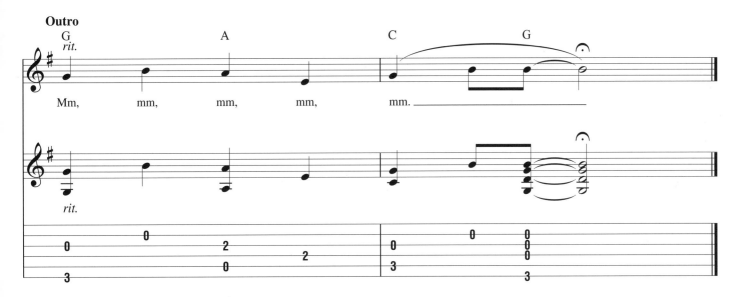

You've Got to Hide Your Love Away

Words and Music by John Lennon and Paul McCartney

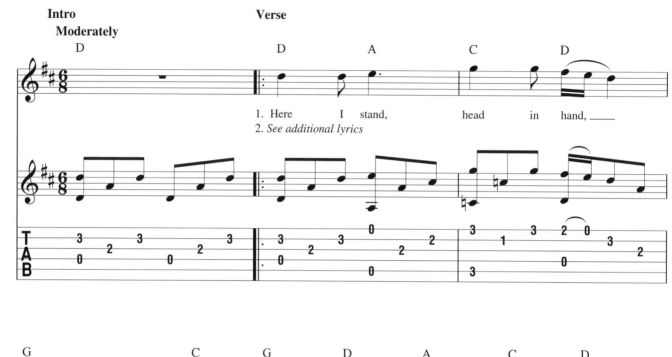

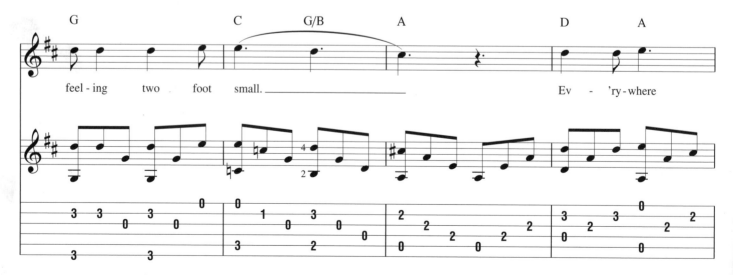

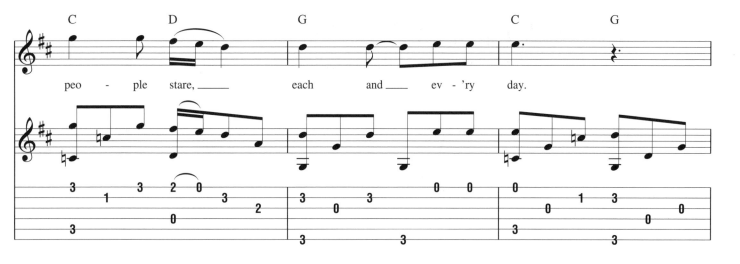

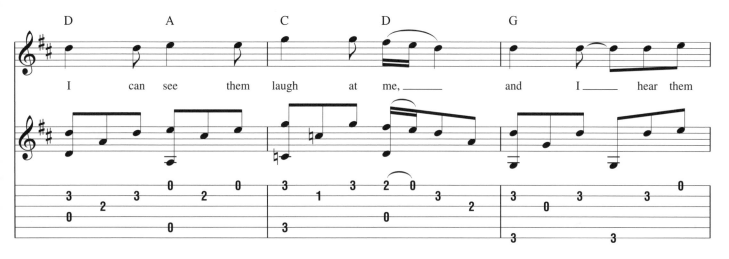

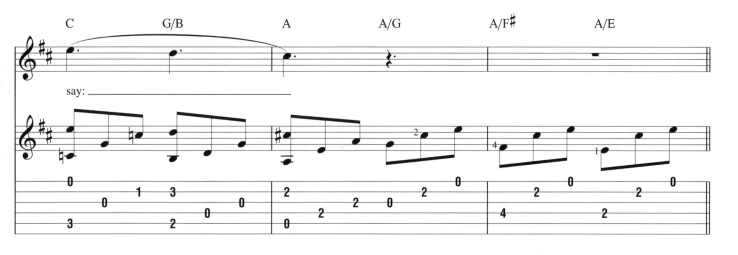

Chorus

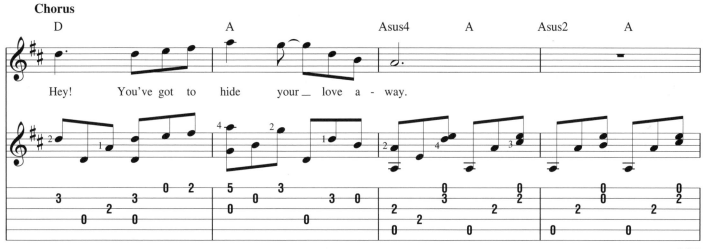

Hey! You've got to hide your love a - way.

Outro

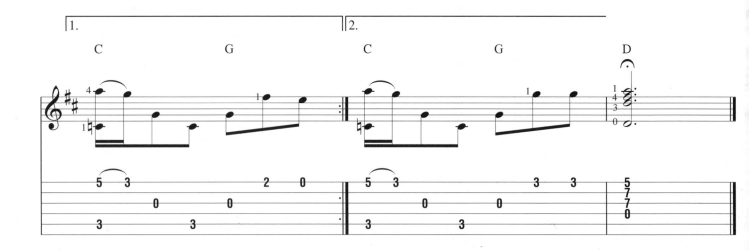

Additional Lyrics

2. How could I even try, I can never win.
   Hearing them, seeing them, in the state I'm in.
   How could she say to me love will find a way?
   Gather round all you clowns, let me hear you say: